The Freedom Doctrine

The Architecture for Global Freedom

- *Relating, Empowering, Freeing*

- *Interdependent Cultural Relating*

- *Free Enterprise Economics*

- *Direct Democratic Government*

- *New Capital Development*

Robert R. Carkhuff, Ph.D., Bernard G. Berenson, Ph.D. and Associates

Published by: Possibilities Publishing
                 22 Amherst Road
                 Amherst, MA 01002
                 800-822-2801 (U.S. and Canada)
                 413-253-3488
                 413-253-3490 (fax)
                 www.FreedomDoctrine.org
                 www.Nation-Building.org
                 www.Carkhuff.com
                 www.HRDPress.com
                 Printed in Canada

ISBN 0-87425-742-5

Editorial services by Mary George
Production services by Jean Miller
Cover design by Eileen Klockars

The Freedom Doctrine:
The Architecture for Global Freedom

D. D. Anderson, I. Conrad, C. Littlefield, S. Mackler, R. Muise
American International College

W. Anthony, M. Cohen, M. Farkas, C. Gagne
Boston University

D. M. Benoit, R. Bierman, G. Oliver, S. Kelly, J. Tamagini
Carkhuff Thinking Systems, Inc.

C. J. Carkhuff, R. Bellingham, W. Epstein, T. W. Friel
The Possibilities Organization Project

D. N. Aspy, C. B. Aspy, J. Barnet, F. N. Roebuck
The Possibilities Education Project

G. Banks, K. Banks, J. A. Linder, G. Logan-El, J. Pope
The Possibilities Community Project

S. Fisher, A. Douds, D. C. Meyers, R. M. Pierce, D. Stanley
Human Technology, Inc.

J. R. Cannon, A. A. Cook, T. W. Friel, H. Oyarzabal
The New Capital Development Group

A. H. Griffin, L. Goodstein, J. Drasgow, J. T. Kelly, R. Owen
Freedom Doctrine International

> *"Where there is no vision,
> the people cast off restraint."*
>
> – King Solomon, *Proverbs* 29:18

Table of Contents

About the Creators of
The Freedom Doctrine

ROBERT R. CARKHUFF, PH.D., is C.E.O., **Freedom Doctrine International,** and Founder and Chairperson of **The Carkhuff Group of Corporations.** One of the most-cited social scientists of our time according to **The Institute for Scientific Information,** Carkhuff is author of several of the most-referenced books of the 20th century, including the two-volume *Helping and Human Relations.* He is visionary creator (with Bernard G. Berenson) of *The New Science of Possibilities* and architect of the **New Capital Development** and **Freedom-Building Systems** upon which is based *The Freedom Doctrine—The Architecture for Global Freedom.*

BERNARD G. BERENSON, PH.D., is Chairman, **Freedom Doctrine International,** and Executive Director, **Carkhuff Institute of Human Technology and Applied Science.** Co-founder (along with Dr. Carkhuff and Dr. Andrew H. Griffin) of the first **Center for Human Resource Development** at **American International College** in 1968, he is also author of *The Possibilities Mind* and visionary of **The Philosophy of Possibilities Science** upon which *The New Science of Possibilities* and *The Freedom Doctrine* are based.

About the Contributors

Carkhuff and Berenson have called for *"possibilities thinkers"*: new *"human processors"* whom they label *"scientist-biographers"*:

- People who transform static content into dynamic processes by processing interdependently with all phenomena—human and otherwise;

- People who commit ideation to the biography of continuously changing phenomena that, in turn, generate their own changeable destinies.

We aspire humbly to become *"scientist-biographers"*!

Debbie D. Anderson, D.Ed.
Director, Center for Human
  Resource Development,
American International College

William Anthony, Ph.D.
Director, Center for Psychiatric
  Rehabilitation
Boston University

Cheryl B. Aspy, D.Ed.
The Possibilities Education,
Carkhuff Thinking Systems, Inc.

David N. Aspy, D.Ed.
The Possibilities Education,
Carkhuff Thinking Systems, Inc.

George Banks, Ph.D.
The Possibilities Community,
Carkhuff Thinking Systems, Inc.

Karen Banks, Ph.D.
The Possibilities Community,
Carkhuff Thinking Systems, Inc.

James Barnet, M.A.
The Possibilities Education,
Carkhuff Thinking Systems, Inc.

Rick Bellingham, Ph.D.
The Possibilities Organization,
Carkhuff Thinking Systems, Inc.

Donald M. Benoit, M.Ed.
Director, Human and Information
  R&D,
Carkhuff Thinking Systems, Inc.

Ralph Bierman, Ph.D.
The Possibilities Community,
Carkhuff Thinking Systems, Inc.

John R. Cannon, Ph.D.
C.E.O.,
Human Technology, Inc.

Christopher J. Carkhuff, M.A. Cert.
The Possibilities Organization,
Carkhuff Thinking Systems, Inc.

Mikal Cohen, Ph.D.
Sargent College of Health,
Boston University

Irving Conrad, D.Ed.,
Administration,
American International College

Alvin A. Cook, Ph.D.
C.O.O.,
Freedom Doctrine International

Al Douds, M.S.W.
Performance Management,
Human Technology, Inc.

James Drasgow, Ph.D.
Department of Psychology (Emeritus),
State University of New York
   at Buffalo

Warren Epstein, M.A.
The Possibilities Organization,
Carkhuff Thinking Systems, Inc.

Mariane Farkas, Sc.D.
Sargent College of Health,
Boston University

Sharon Fisher, M.Ed.
C.O.O.,
Human Technology, Inc.

Ted W. Friel, Ph.D.
Economic Capital Development,
The New Capital Development
   Group

Cheryl Gagne, M.A.
Sargent College of Health,
Boston University

Leonard D. Goodstein, Ph.D.
Former C.E.O.,
American Psychological Association

Andrew H. Griffin, D.Ed.
Assistant Superintendent,
Washington Office of Education

John T. Kelly, D.Sc.
Advanced Systems Development
(Emeritus), IBM, Inc.

Susan Kelly, B.A.
Manager, Customer Services,
IBM, Inc.

John A. Linder, D.Sc.
The Possibilities Community,
Carkhuff Thinking Systems, Inc.

Cindy Littlefield, M.A., C.A.G.S.
Center for Human Resource
   Development,
American International College

George Logan-El, Ph.D.
The Possibilities Community,
Carkhuff Thinking Systems, Inc.

Susan Mackler, M.A., C.A.G.S.
Director, Computer Science,
Holyoke Community College

David Meyers, M.A.
Organizational Systems,
Human Technology, Inc.

Richard Muise, M.A., C.A.G.S.
Center for Human Resource
   Development,
American International College

Gerald Oliver, D.Sc.
The Possibilities Community,
Carkhuff Thinking Systems, Inc.

Rob Owen, M.B.A.
President,
Freedom Doctrine International

Hernan Oyarzabal, B.A.
Executive Director, Spain and
   Central America,
International Monetary Fund

Richard Pierce, Ph.D.
Human Resource Management,
Human Technology, Inc.

John Pope, M.Ed.
UNITY Project,
Washington Office of Education

Flora N. Roebuck, D.Ed.
The Possibilities Education,
Carkhuff Thinking Systems, Inc.

Dennis Stanley, M.A.
Organization Systems,
Human Technology, Inc.

Jeannette Tamagini, D.Ed.
The Possibilities Community,
Carkhuff Thinking Systems, Inc.

We dedicate our work to the greatest and most powerful application of
Possibilities Science: *The Freedom Doctrine—The Architecture for Global
Freedom.*

The Scientist-Biographers
Human Resource Development Press
Amherst, Massachusetts

PREFACE
The Freedom Doctrine

by J. R. Cannon, Ph.D.
Executive Editor
C.E.O., Human Technology, Inc.

For scientists, freedom is a function of our response repertoires: the more responses, the more freedom. Indeed, without the responses, we cannot even discriminate the opportunity for their use.

For the possibilities scientists, freedom is a function of our repertoires of processing, or thinking, responses: the more thinking responses, the more freedom. With these processing responses, we can generate our own degrees of freedom.

Our processing-response repertoires are thus critical to freedom, and freedom is critical to them:

- They define our ability to relate freely to all experiences, people, and even nations — **our social freedom!**

- They require a free market environment to which we may apply them freely — **our economic freedom!**

- They require the political power to use them freely — **our political freedom!**

Essentially, freedom is found in our ability to think and to generate new and more productive responses to the changing conditions of our times in socially, economically, and politically free environments!

Just as we produce free individuals by empowering them with free thinking responses, so do we produce free nations by empowering them with free processing responses. For nations and cultures, these responses have to do with the development of freedom's resources:

- **Socially** empowered responses that enable **cultural relating;**

- **Economically** empowered responses that enable **economic enterprise;**

- **Politically** empowered responses that enable **supportive governance.**

In short, the empowerment of freedom's resources provides the conditions for empowering and freeing individuals as well as cultures and nations.

In Table 1, we may view **The Freedom Doctrine. The Freedom Architecture** that guides the development of **The Freedom Doctrine** will be presented in this body of work.

Table 1. The Freedom Doctrine

I.	To lead freely by relating, empowering, and freeing all peoples dedicated to participating in our integrated and elevated global society;
II.	To relate freely and interdependently with all cultures dedicated to growing in our global society;
III.	To trade freely and reciprocally in a free enterprise marketplace dedicated to mutual growth in our global society;
IV.	To govern freely and democratically within, between, and among all nations in our global society;
V.	To empower our communities freely to generate all forms of new capital in order to produce a spiraling array of products, services, and solutions that benefit all humankind.

The book, itself, is divided into four main sections:

I. *Introduction and Overview.* This section focuses on the processing systems that constitute the scientific methods at the foundation of all freedom and, thus, all civilization.

II. *The New Capital Development Systems.* These are the systems that empower us to accomplish any human vision. They are the generating engine for **Freedom-Building.**

III. *The Freedom-Building Systems.* These define the ingredients for building free peoples and nations in the 21st Century.

IV. *Summary and Transition.* This section presents **The Freedom Doctrine,** which prescribes the architecture for global freedom in the 21st Century.

Eager readers may skip ahead to Chapter 13, which provides more detailed information on **The Freedom Doctrine.** They may then go back and fill in their understanding of the ingredients necessary for elevating and integrating civilization in the 21st century.

The global need for **The Freedom Doctrine** is well illustrated in Figure 1; this figure also points to a basic thesis of this work—that we can define freedom and assess its effects on performance. As may be viewed, **Free Nations** perform significantly different than **Unfree Nations** on *all* indices of performance:

- **Cultural Relating**
- **Economic Prosperity**
- **Supportive Governance**

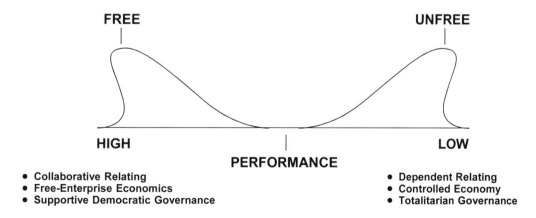

Figure 1. The Performance Curves of Free and Unfree Nations

The curves themselves represent separate and distinct categories of nations. **Free Nations** are culturally relating, economically prosperous, and governmentally supportive. In short, **Free Nations** are **"free"**: culturally, economically, governmentally. **Unfree Nations** are simply not free! **There is no overlap between the curves!**

Other nations should have no conflict in choosing their future directions. This is not a philosophical discussion. **The Freedom Doctrine** is there for all to study and observe.

FOREWORD
The Great Experiments

by Rob Owen, M.B.A.
President,
Freedom Doctrine International

In the history of humankind, there have been three great movements in freedom for civilization and its people. Each constitutes a vital experiment in the realization of human potential.

The First Experiment—Ancient Greece

The first freedom movement was embodied in the government of Pericles in ancient Greece. Schooled in the writings of Greek philosophers such as Plato and Aristotle, Pericles demonstrated that true democracy was possible. Although his demonstration was fatally flawed by the system of slavery upon which Greek democracy was based, it was an initial step toward a new view of government and citizenry. As such, it was **The First Experiment in Freedom.** And it was validated!

The Great Experiment—The United States

The second great movement was the American system, founded more than 200 years ago. Basing their ideas upon the work of European philosophers such as John Locke, Thomas Hobbes, and David Hume, the founders of this system demonstrated that not only democratic governance was possible, but free enterprise economics as well.

Of course, the American system was also flawed by withholding full freedoms and rights from First Americans, women, blacks, and other marginalized peoples. However, this flaw was not a fatal one. Our founders were politically conscious enough to give us an amending instrument to enact changes in the movement toward full freedom: the U.S. Constitution. The equality of all "men" having been declared, it remained for the disenfranchised to seek and achieve their own civil and human rights through amendments to the Constitution.

Indeed, today the U.S. stands alone as the beacon of freedom in the world:

- Its 50 states, some of them larger than countries, live together peacefully and productively in the freest social system the world has ever known.

- Its 50 states, many of which would be among the most prosperous of countries, conduct the freest and most powerful wealth-generating economic system in the history of the world.

- The citizens of its 50 states are constitutionally the policymakers of the freest representative democratic governance of the most powerful nation in the history of the world.

The U.S. has truly demonstrated itself to be **The Great Experiment.** And it has been validated!

The Next Great Experiment—Free Global Society

Evolving in our times, the third freedom movement is represented by **The Freedom Doctrine,** which offers a futuristic vision of the global village and its marketplace. Informed by the spiraling achievements of the American experiment, **The Freedom Doctrine** points civilization toward an elevated and integrated global society based upon the fundamental proposition of **Global Freedom:** *"All nations are created equal in their potential for freedom."* The functions of such freedom include:

- **Free and interdependent cultural relating,**
- **Entrepreneurially driven, free enterprise economics,**
- **Free and direct democratic governance.**

The methods for achieving these **Freedom Functions** tell the story of **The Freedom Doctrine.**

We are thus called to engage in **The Next Great Experiment**—to build our people, our communities, all cultures, and all nations into an elevated, integrated, and interdependent global society. This is **The Freedom Doctrine,** and it will be validated again and again.

PROLOG
The Freedom-Builders
by David N. Aspy, D.Ed.

In the 1950s, as a budding scientist, I was privileged to work at the University of Chicago in the very same place where Enrico Fermi and his researchers had conducted the first successful tests of atomic chain reaction. There I was fortunate enough to participate in conferences with Robert Oppenheimer and his group of distinguished scientists, all of who were instrumental in saving us from catastrophe in the Second World War.

During discussions, Oppenheimer himself would usually listen intently. On the rare occasions when he did speak, his manner and words were to the point. He would quickly specify the issue at hand and present his views in precise language, formulae, and equations. This fit the atmosphere of the conferences, one permeated with a sense of "scientific protocol."

Communication in this environment was typically restrictive, limited to a conservative scientific point of view. Remarks "outside the box" of orthodox science were simply ignored. It was comparable to being at a world-class chess match: everyone knew the rules and adhered to them rigidly; moves outside those strictures were such "bad form" that they were beneath comment and, indeed, contempt.

The basic assumption here was quite simple: that everything could be described, predicted, and controlled by the conceptual tools available to scientists. This assumption, which summarizes the rules—or more properly, the functions—of probabilities science, fed a persistent, exclusive perspective on phenomena, science included. The search for new technologies, tools, and "gadgets" might be admissible, but questioning the *perspective itself* was a different matter. There was an absence of the notion that whole new operational perspectives of science were possible. The prevailing attitude was that all of the major questions had been answered. These scientists believed that because they had tested their findings, they had validated their privileged access to the ultimate power of the universe.

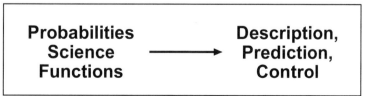

Of course, we were living in a postwar world where science was widely credited with having saved millions of lives by forcing, through atomic means, the surrender of Japan. Atomic energy was considered the force of the future, and world peace maintained by fear of atomic warfare. The scene was one of ego-centered satisfaction with the status quo. It was thought there was nowhere else to go: science had proved its potency by parenting the ultimate child.

In the 1960s, my journey took a new course, into processing, guided by Carkhuff and Berenson and their associates. In an old mill overlooking a waterfall in Massachusetts, they introduced me to the limitless power of our brains to generate our own destinies. Open inquiry with systematic interdependent processing was the hallmark of my meetings with them.

Unlike the rigidly structured conferences in Chicago, those meetings were informal and permeated by a learning spirit. Their freedom was shaped by systematic processes for generating new and more powerful images of phenomena:

- *Exploring* our images of current phenomena by analyzing the operations of the phenomena;

- *Understanding* new images of the phenomena by synthesizing more powerful operations;

- *Acting* upon these more powerful images of the phenomena by operationalizing new objectives and technologizing programs to achieve the objectives.

These processes, **E-U-A,** defined our "method." We used them to generate *"best ideas."* The latter were provisional: they governed our processing until we generated even better ideas.

By redefining processing, Carkhuff and Berenson redefined the terms of science. They replaced controlling functions with relating functions. They added empowering functions through the newly generated processing systems: people could thus be empowered to generate their own new and powerful ideation. These scientists were now on the verge of their most profound discoveries.

Empowerment in generative processing enabled not only interdependent phenomenal processing, but also the nesting and freeing of all phenomenal systems. Carkhuff and Berenson defined phenomena generically in terms of their operations and, in so doing, generated the principles of changeability that account for the evolution of phenomena. Among them:

- Unequality in processing potential;

- Nesting in more powerful, higher-order phenomenal processing systems;

- Sociogenetic coding of lower-order processing systems by higher-order systems;

- Continuous rotating of processing systems to higher- or lower-order functions.

These principles define continuous interdependent processing. They define changeability. They define freedom as the highest-order function in **The New Science of Possibilities.**

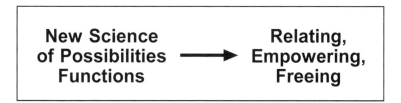

In this context, we are blessed with *possibilities science.* Released by its own freeing function, it addresses the great issues of our times—most notably, culture change and movement toward an integrated global village and its marketplace. It is truly an awesome *construct system* dedicated to the advancement of 21st century civilization in all of its expressions. All of this is not to say that *probabilities science* did not make enormous contributions. It did and we were all proud to be part of it. However, trapped by its controlling function, we were limited in our 20th century perspective of stasis; moreover, when frustrated, we retreated to the holocaustic weaponry of an awesome *destruct system.*

In summary, it is the privilege of my lifetime in science, education, and cultural development to introduce the true **"Freedom-Builders":** Robert R. Carkhuff and Bernard G. Berenson and their associates. Their work will carry out *The Promise of America,* serving as the pilot project for **The Freedom Doctrine — The Architecture for Global Freedom** for a peaceful, productive, and prosperous planet.

My life's journey thus continues — in the changeable moment, in the realm of possibilities! There are processing systems to relate to the wonders of phenomena, multidimensional and asymmetrical models to represent the changeable nature of our universes, and infinite and continuing interdependent intelligence to be found in God's work. Carkhuff and Berenson have made these possibilities known to us.

I. Introduction and Overview

1. Processing — The Methods of Science
by James Drasgow, Ph.D.

Processing—The Methods of Science
MEANING

For millions of years, people functioned primarily in terms of conditioned responding. Then, with the *Agrarian* and *Industrial Ages*, people began to use discriminative learning processes. Now, with the introduction of the *Information Age* and the emerging *Age of Ideation*, people are learning to process generatively, creating responses that were heretofore unknown.

Freedom requires thinking or processing. Conditioned responders are unfree. They are followers—controlled by their limited responses. Discriminative learners are less than free. They are limited by the responses they can find. Only thinking people are truly free—generating their own ideas and their own futures.

This chapter is essential for understanding freedom by helping us understand the methods of science—*"Possibilities Science"*—that enable generative processing.

"I am quite convinced that someone will come up with a theory whose objects, connected by laws, are not probabilities."
— Einstein, 1956

I believe that Carkhuff and Berenson are that "someone" to whom Einstein was referring. In their own "mental laboratories," these scientists have related, empowered, and freed all phenomenological systems *"to seek their own changeable destinies."* They have defined *Possibilities Science* as contra-distinguished from our historic *Probabilities Science.* Accordingly, they have positioned the processing systems of possibilities to generate and drive the planning systems of probabilities.

Clearly, Carkhuff and Berenson fit this definition as exemplary performers. But there is more. Not only do these scientists provide us with the processes for explicating phenomena, they also empower us with processes for generating *new* phenomena. Witness, for example, the first multidimensional models for community, governance, economics, and culture that were generated as extensions of their now-powerful new capital development (NCD) systems: marketplace, organization, human, information, and mechanical.

This generative processing power of **The New Science of Possibilities** is evident in the many dynamic models, systems, and technologies presented to us by these scientists. Indeed, Carkhuff and Berenson have validated possibilities science by offering the first *"prepotent demonstration of master organic-engineering architecture"*: **The Science of All New Sciences!**

In this context, the present work introduces **The New Science of Possibilities** and its applications in **New Capital Development (NCD)** and **Freedom-Building:**

- *The Relating Sciences* that provide a platform for all **NCD** (Chapter 2);

- *The Information Sciences* that define all **NCD** (Chapter 3);

- *The Human Sciences* that empower all **NCD** (Chapter 4);

- *The Organizational Sciences* that position and align resources for all **NCD** (Chapter 5);

- *The Community-Building Sciences* that empower the community to become the generating engine for all **Freedom-Building** (Chapter 6);

- *The Freedom Functions* that define **Freedom-Building** (Chapter 7);

- *The NCD Components* that enable **Freedom-Building** (Chapter 8);

- *The Freedom-Building Sciences* that define culture with emerging new capital ingredients, (Chapter 9);

- *The Freedom-Building Sciences* that define the health and wealth of our nations (Chapter 10);

- *The Freedom-Building Sciences* that enable globalization (Chapter 11);

- *The Freedom-Building Sciences* that empower American leadership (Chapter 12);

- *The Freedom-Building Sciences* that culminate in **The Freedom Doctrine** (Chapter 13).

"Best Processes"

Let us start with an image of *"best practices."* The private and public sector alike are built upon *"best practices"* — the practices that have evolved and have been validated as *"tried and true"* by the best minds of our time. The problem is that *"best practices"* **do not work,** for one overriding reason: *"things change!"* Such practices simply do not respond to the changing conditions of our times. Carkhuff and Berenson put it this way: *"By the time we have trained responses in best practices, the conditions have changed and the practices are no longer 'best!'"*

Conditioned Responding

Carkhuff and Berenson put the category of *"all practices"* in learning-theory terms. They view *all practices* — from people making machine-like responses in learning/work situations to cultures preserving ritualistic traditions that once had meaning — in terms of **conditioned responding** (see Figure 1-1). Here the relatively stable complex of stimulus conditions **(S)** prompt reflexive, *knee-jerk* responses **(R).**

$$S \longrightarrow s-r-s-r \longrightarrow R$$

Figure 1-1. Conditioned Responding

Although conditioned responding is generally considered *"untouched by human brainpower,"* there are actually spinally conditioned, anticipatory — or *"chained"* — responses intervening between **S** and **R: s–r–s–r.** Primitive cultures continue to be dominated by such conditioning.

Discriminative Learning

It is to the representatives of the next class of processing that we make most awards. This is the category of branching systems, or *"decision trees,"* that define the ***"best practices"*** of our times. Carkhuff and Berenson view ***"best practices"*** in terms of **discriminative learning** (see Figure 1-2). Here the changing complex of stimuli **(S)** are processed by the human organism **(O)** to make the appropriate responses **(R).**

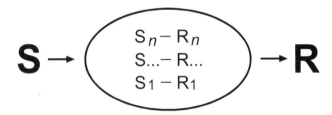

Figure 1-2. Discriminative Learning

As we may see, the human organism is the repository of a repertoire of ***"S–R conditioned responses."*** The organism simply discriminates the relevant characteristics of the stimulus and selects and emits the appropriate response. While advanced cultures are, themselves, learning to process in discriminative-learning terms, the stimulus conditions are changing so rapidly that the repertoires of conditioned responses are no longer appropriate. While prizes are awarded in this category, the contributions and, hence, the contributors tend to become *"retarders"* of progress rather than *"facilitators"* of it.

Generative Thinking

The next class of processing responses is where Carkhuff and Berenson exhibit the creativity that deserves recognition. Beyond *"expert systems,"* this is a category that defines the capability to generate new and more powerful responses that, in turn, define the ***"best ideas"*** of our times. In this context, the scientists differentiate ideas from practices in the same manner that they distinguish leaders from followers or initiators from imitators. Carkhuff and Berenson, then, view ***"best ideas"*** in terms of **generative thinking** (see Figure 1-3). Here the spiraling changes in stimulus conditions **(S)** are processed by human processors **(P)** to generate entirely new responses **(R).**

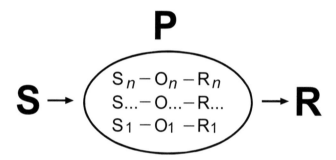

Figure 1-3. Generative Thinking

As we can see, the human processor incorporates a repertoire of *"S–O–R discriminative learning"* responses: the processor utilizes permutations and combinations of these responses to generate entirely new responses that the stimuli were not calculated to elicit. Indeed, the human processor actually contributes new standards to the requirements of the continuously changing stimulus conditions. Surely, no prizes are awarded here because the generative contributions — not innovative transfers — are *beyond the high beams* of selection committees and consensus criteria.

Nested Processing Systems

In creating the generative thinking systems, Carkhuff and Berenson have built upon the historic contributions of their mentors in conditioning and learning, scientists such as Bugelski, Hull, and Mowrer. This is well illustrated in Figure 1-4.

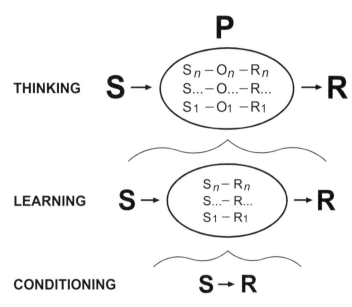

Figure 1-4. The Nesting of Processing Systems

Here, the **S–R** conditioning systems are *nested* in the *S–O–R learning systems;* in turn, the *S–O–R systems* are *nested* in the *S–P–R thinking systems.* By *housing* the systems in this manner, Carkhuff and Berenson contributed the first comprehensive systems description of human processing.

Along with several associates, Carkhuff and Berenson built upon human processing systems to generate all manner of processing systems. They began this stage of their work with **Organizational Processing** systems (see Figure 1-5). As may be viewed, the human processing systems are *nested* in the organizational processing systems. The latter have their own unique processing contributions, as we will discover later.

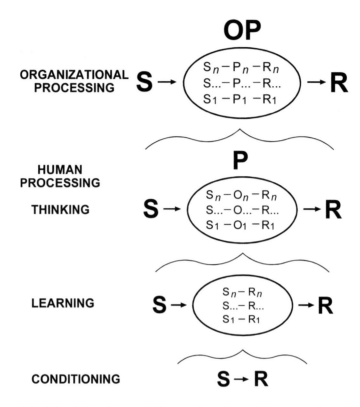

Figure 1-5. The Nesting of Organizational Processing Systems

With several other associates, these scientists generated all manner of **Phenomenal Processing** systems (see Figure 1-6). As we may note, the phenomenal processing systems are represented generically. In this way, they represent the uniqueness of all processing systems: mechanical, informational, human, organizational, marketplace, community, governance, economic, and cultural.

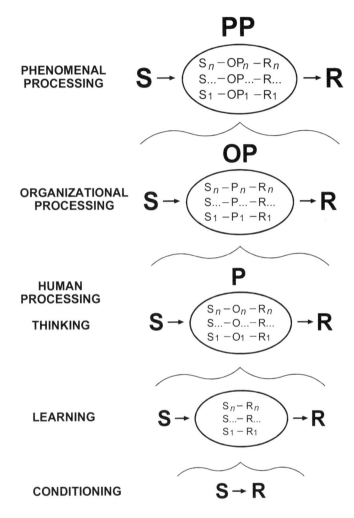

Figure 1-6. The Nesting of Phenomenal Processing Systems

These breakthroughs enabled the creation of the generative processing systems that lead to *"best processes." Best processes* are the generative processes with which we relate to the phenomena we are addressing. We utilize our substantive knowledge of phenomenal processing systems to process interdependently with the phenomena.

The big breakthroughs came to Carkhuff and Berenson with *virtual processing*. This enabled them to align processing with some of the critical ingredients of all phenomena:

- All phenomena are *nested* in higher-order phenomena.

- All phenomena are sociogenetically *encoded* by higher-order phenomena.

- All phenomena *rotate* to become higher-order phenomena.

This means that all phenomena are continuously *nesting, encoding,* and *rotating* in relation to other phenomena.

Empowered by these and other ingredients, Carkhuff and Berenson went on to generate **The New Science of Possibilities,** a science that makes all things possible:

- By aligning to *relate* to phenomena;

- By intervening to *empower* phenomena;

- By releasing to *free* phenomena.

These basic possibilities principles enable all phenomena to seek their own changeable destinies.

For Carkhuff and Berenson, everything is processing. All phenomena are continuously processing and, in doing so, are continuously changing. Unlike their probabilities-science brethren, they are not confined by static content—there is no such thing. Content is merely stimulus input to be processed to generate yet another content response.

The implications for human brainpower are as profound as hominids assuming *the upright posture.* We can make our brain structures bigger and stronger and empower our neurons to *bridge neuronal gaps.* We can empower our brains to process fully our entire environment—internal and external—rather than the three square meters of dust before us. We can live with our brains growing continuously and incrementally. We can die growing!

In summary, *best processes* empower all of us to address the major issues of our time—perhaps forever! *Best processes* are the foundation for our freedom!

References

Berenson, B. G. and Carkhuff, R. R. *The Possibilities Mind.* Amherst, MA: HRD Press, 2001.

Bugelski, B. R. *The Psychology of Learning.* New York: Holt, Rinehart & Winston, 1956.

Carkhuff, R. R. *Sources of Human Productivity.* Amherst, MA: HRD Press, 1983.

Carkhuff, R. R. *The Exemplar.* Amherst, MA: HRD Press, 1984.

Carkhuff, R. R. *Human Processing and Human Productivity.* Amherst, MA: HRD Press, 1986.

Carkhuff, R. R. *Human Possibilities.* Amherst, MA: HRD Press, 2000.

Carkhuff, R. R. and Berenson, B. G. *The New Science of Possibilities. Volume I. The Processing Science.* Amherst, MA: HRD Press, 2000.

Carkhuff, R. R. and Berenson, B. G. *The New Science of Possibilities. Volume II. The Processing Technologies.* Amherst, MA: HRD Press, 2000.

Carkhuff, R. R. and Berenson, B. G. *Possibilities Thinking.* Amherst, MA: HRD Press, 2002.

Carkhuff, R. R. and Berenson, B. G. *The Principles of Possibilities Science.* Amherst, MA: HRD Press, 2002.

Hull, C. L. *Essentials of Behavior.* New Haven: Yale University Press, 1951.

Mowrer, O. H. *Learning Theory and the Symbolic Processes.* New York: J. Wiley, 1960.

II. The New Capital Development Systems

2. Relating—The Precondition of Possibilities

by William Anthony, Ph.D.
Cheryl B. Aspy, D.Ed.
Ralph Bierman, Ph.D.
Mikal Cohen, Ph.D.
Marianne Farkas, Sc.D.
Cheryl Gagne, M.A.
Flora N. Roebuck, D.Ed.
Jeannette Tamagini, D.Ed.

Relating—The Precondition of Possibilities

MEANING

Relating is the foundation for all *New Capital Development*. Indeed, it is the foundation of all civilization: it is reciprocity in relating that enables civilization.

Without "skilled relating" people, organizations, and even nations are trapped within themselves. With "skilled relating" they are freed to "process" or "think-through" mutually beneficial solutions to problems and opportunities. Relating brings people—and the organizations and nations they represent—together. Yet, despite the essential role of skilled relating at every level of human contact—person to person, business to business, nation to nation—we do not tend to employ relating skills in our own actions!

This chapter will orient us to essential models and methods of relating to help individuals, organizations, and even nations to relate and inter-relate.

Many people remember Robert R. Carkhuff and Bernard G. Berenson for their early work in helping and human relating. The plain fact is that these scientists have devoted their lives to helping:

- First helping individuals and groups,
- Then helping organizations and communities,
- Now helping economies and cultures.

They have run the gamut of human experience. Moreover, they have expanded the parameters of human experience.

For Carkhuff and Berenson, **relating**—from its initial interpersonal form to its ultimate interdependent form—has been the core of human experience: indeed, the human requirement. Before people can help others, they must enter the others' frames of reference. For these scientists, the basic principle in helping was the principle of learning:

All learning begins with the learner's frame of reference.

They extended the learning principle into all areas of human endeavor:

All learning is instrumental for individual purposes.

They culminated the learning principle in a guiding insight for all human experience:

All learning culminates in achievement of the skills objective.

With these breakthrough principles, all possibilities of teaching and learning were generated. Along with them, the science of possibilities for all phenomena—human and otherwise—was born:

- **Relating to phenomenal experience,**
- **Empowering the potential of phenomena,**
- **Freeing the phenomena to actualize their own changeable destinies.**

Relating Research and Development

The research and development began with the breakthrough insight of the *"interchangeability of responding"*:

> *Could one person (the helper) have communicated what the other person (the helpee) had communicated in terms of the feeling and meaning and the content of the expression?*

The interchangeable response enabled Carkhuff and Berenson to assess the effectiveness of all helping and human relationships.

What they discovered was astounding. Some helpers — parents, teachers, counselors, managers — never made an interchangeable response — never, ever! How, then, could they help others achieve their objectives? Other helpers — less than five of 100 — would periodically check back with their helpees by making interchangeable responses.

The outcomes followed the processes. The helpees of helpers who made interchangeable responses improved on a whole variety of indices. The helpees of the *"helpers"* who did not make interchangeable responses stayed the same or even declined on a variety of indices.

Again: *all learning begins with the learner's frame of reference.*

The ingredients of interpersonal relating evolved as Carkhuff and Berenson conducted further research in response to a number of challenges to the helping profession. In the process, they became among the first to find that helping may be *"for better or for worse,"* that is, facilitative or retarding — a finding with significant implications for parents, teachers, counselors, therapists, managers, and the like. Moreover, Carkhuff and Berenson also discovered that they could account for the facilitative or retarding effects by the helpers' levels of functioning on certain scaled dimensions, such as empathic relating or responding.

It is worthwhile to view the models of relating that evolved through living, learning, and working applications associated with this research.

The Relating Models

The main effect of empathic relating on the part of the helper was to facilitate exploration of experience on the part of the helpee. With that, the researchers had their first model for helping: *helper responding facilitates the helpee's experiential exploring of problems* (Figure 2-1).

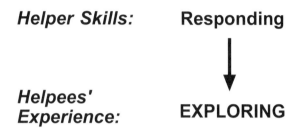

Figure 2-1. Early Model for Helping

Eclectically drawing upon all theoretical orientations, Carkhuff and Berenson explored many scaled dimensions and then factor-analyzed them. They discovered that these dimensions "loaded" upon two discrete interpersonal factors:

- Responding that emphasized empathy, respect, and warmth in relating to other people's frames of reference;

- Initiating that emphasized genuineness, concreteness, and self-disclosure of the helper's own experiences.

With that, the researchers had a basic model for helping (Figure 2-2):

- *Responding facilitates exploring.*
- *Initiating stimulates acting.*

The helpees could now act upon their explorations of experience.

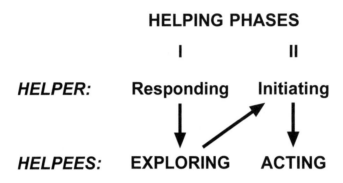

Figure 2-2. Basic Model for Helping

Further requirements of the interpersonal dimensions yielded a transitional dimension between responding and initiating, based on the personalizing factor:

- Personalizing that emphasized immediacy of experiencing, confrontation, and internalizing, especially as it relates to responsibility for one's actions.

With that, the researchers had a transitional model for helping (Figure 2-3):

- *Personalizing facilitates understanding.*

The helpees could now act based upon their self-understanding.

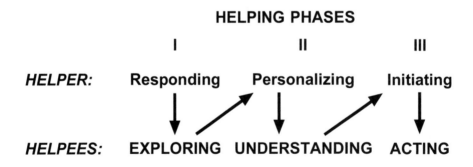

Figure 2-3. Transitional Model for Helping

The comprehensive model was not completed until other factors were analyzed and incorporated. Foremost among these factors was attending:

- Attending that emphasizes paying attention to others by attending physically, observing their appearance and behavior, and listening to their expressions of their experience.

With that, the researchers had a comprehensive model for engaging or involving others in the helping process (Figure 2-4):

- *Attending facilitates involving.*
- *Responding facilitates exploring.*
- *Personalizing facilitates understanding.*
- *Initiating facilitates acting.*

The helpers could now engage the helpees in a comprehensive helping process.

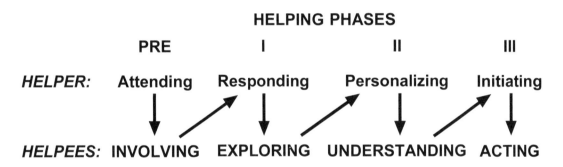

Figure 2-4. Comprehensive Model for Helping

Finally, feedback is recycled for continuous and improved processing (Figure 2-5):

- More intensive involving,
- More extensive exploring,
- More accurate understanding,
- More effective acting.

Both helpees and helpers now had a comprehensive model for continuous processing of increasingly productive responses.

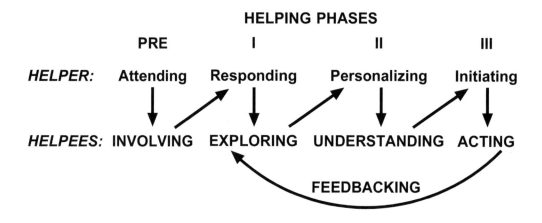

Figure 2-5. Continuous Processing Model for Helping

Learning

With educational applications and analyses, the helping model was expanded to incorporate teaching skills (Figure 2-6). As we may see:

- Content development plus attending facilitates involving.
- Diagnosing plus responding facilitates exploring.
- Learning objectives plus personalizing facilitates understanding.
- Individualizing learning programs plus initiating facilitates acting.

Again, feedback is recycled to facilitate a more productive teaching-learning process. Both teachers and learners could now implement a comprehensive model for learning.

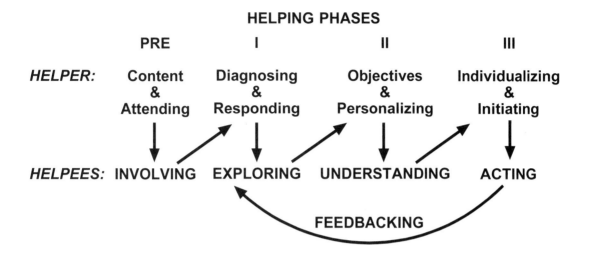

Figure 2-6. Comprehensive Model for Teaching

Working

With working applications and analyses, the helping/teaching model was expanded to incorporate working and thinking skills (Figure 2-7). As we may see:

- Goaling plus content and attending facilitates involving.

- Expanding plus diagnosing and responding facilitates exploring.

- Narrowing plus objectives and personalizing facilitates understanding.

- Programming plus individualizing and initiating facilitates acting.

Once again, feedback is recycled to facilitate the most productive working-thinking process. Managers and supervisors and workers now had a comprehensive model for working and thinking on the job.

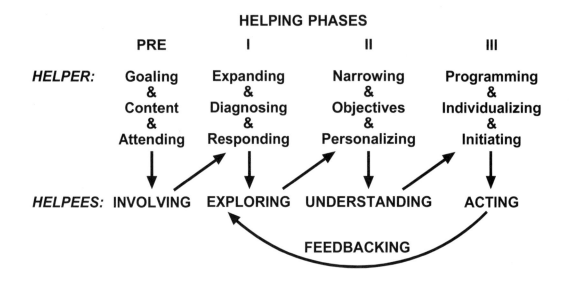

HELPING PHASES

Figure 2-7. Comprehensive Model for Working and Thinking

Carkhuff and Berenson and their associates went on to make demonstrations of the effects of relating interventions in all areas of human experience: parenting, education, counseling, psychotherapy, and business/industry management and supervision.

Moreover, these researchers made demonstrations of the effects of direct relating-skills training upon helpees in all areas of human experience: children, learners, counselees, patients, employees, and supervisees. In doing so, they introduced their principle of *"training as treatment,"* or *"psychological education,"* as a preferred model of treatment. Here is what their research yielded.

Relating Process and Outcome

The effects of interpersonal-skills, or **IPS,** dimensions were summarized by the researchers in a review of 164 studies of more than 160,000 people. In this review, we find several sets of summary propositions drawn from these results as well as their processing-skills implications (Carkhuff, 1983).

Summary Propositions

1. **The effects of helper interpersonal functioning upon recipient outcomes are positive and significant.**
   A summary of the effects of helpers upon helpee outcome indices suggests that interpersonal skills are a core ingredient in any Human Resource Development **(HRD)** effort. Ninety-six percent (96%) of the studies and 92% of the indices yield positive outcomes. Clearly, these helper effects hold across living, learning, and working outcomes.

2. *IPS* **training is the source of high levels of helper interpersonal functioning.**
   In all but ten instances, systematic **IPS** training was the source of helper interpersonal functioning. Thus, in 86% of the studies, **IPS** training was directly related to the effects of helping. That is to say, alone or in combination with other skills, **IPS** training is the significant source of effect in helping efforts.

3. **The effects of direct *IPS* training of recipients upon helpee outcomes are positive and significant.**
   The direct **IPS** training of recipients is a significant source of recipient outcome benefits. In 96% of the studies and 92% of the indices, the reported results were positive. Thus, alone or in combination with other skills, direct **IPS** training of recipients is a potential preferred model of treatment.

4. **Positive results are describable and predictable while negative results are statistical exceptions.**
   Ninety-six percent (96%) of the studies and 92% of the indices had positive outcomes. Thus, putting the issues of rater level of functioning and minimal level of helper functioning aside, it may be concluded that negative result studies and indices tend toward being statistical or random exceptions.

5. **Positive *IPS* outcomes are a consequence of systematic efforts while negative results are design exceptions.**
Systematically derived results involve systematic design: systematic training design, systematic treatment design, systematic follow-up, and systematic environmental support. When present, these ingredients of systematic designs will yield systematic outcomes. When any one of these ingredients is absent, there is an increasing prospect for non-significant or even negative results. Thus, for example, without systematic training, variability in interpersonal functioning will be restricted and the relationships with various outcome indices become problematic.

Processing Skills

In this context, it is extremely important to emphasize IPS as processing skills, alone or in combination with other processing skills [see Table 2-1]. In many of the studies, IPS are employed as the single intervention: the interveners are trained in IPS to intervene with the recipients, or the recipients are trained directly in IPS.

In other studies, IPS are employed in conjunction with other processing skills such as problem-solving or cognitive processing skills.

In summary, the most important issue is the critical nature of interpersonal skills. They serve to enable people to assume the frames of reference of others. They facilitate: the exploration of where others are in relation to a particular experience; the understanding of where others want or need to be; and the action behavior to get from where they are to where they want to be. In this regard, IPS are critical ingredients in the implementation of any programs involving human beings, whether individual, small-group, large-group, or community treatment or training. They may be used in conjunction with any other skills to accomplish any intervention goals involving humans in living, learning, and working performance (Carkhuff, 1983, pp. 82–91).

Table 2-1. A Summary Index of Percentages of Predominantly Positive Results of *IPS* Studies and Indices of Helpee Living, Learning, and Working Outcomes

OUTCOMES	HELPERS	HELPEES	OUTCOMES
LIVING			**LIVING**
Studies (N = 22)	91% Positive	92% Positive	Studies (N = 35)
Indices (N = 117)	83% Positive	83% Positive	Indices (N = 128)
LEARNING			**LEARNING**
Studies (N = 32)	97% Positive	100% Positive	Studies (N = 26)
Indices (N = 261)	92% Positive	99% Positive	Indices (N = 78)
WORKING			**WORKING**
Studies (N = 22)	100% Positive	100% Positive	Studies (N = 27)
Indices (N = 83)	96% Positive	98% Positive	Indices (N = 117)
SUBTOTAL			**SUBTOTAL**
Studies (N = 76)	96% Positive	96% Positive	Studies (N = 88)
Indices (N = 461)	92% Positive	92% Positive	Indices (N = 323)
GRAND TOTAL			
Studies (N = 164)	96% Positive		
Indices (N = 784)	92% Positive		

Carkhuff, 1983, p. 86

Relating Applications and Transfers

The implications for parenting and helping, teaching and training, employing and working are profound. When helpers are trained to relate effectively to all levels within an organization — up and sideways as well as down — then they and their recipients are productive in achieving mutually beneficial goals. Furthermore, when the recipients are trained directly in relating effectively — up, down, and sideways — then they are productive in achieving their goals.

In this context, comprehensive intervention designs have been introduced in the arenas of living, learning, and working skills.

Living

Intervention designs for living include:

- The parenting skills training movement,
- The lay counseling or "functional" professional movement,
- The community-based mental health and medical movements,
- The psychiatric rehabilitation movement,
- The correctional counseling and youth diversion movements,
- *"The Possibilities Helper"* movement.

For example, in the first comprehensive *"Possibilities Helper"* community-based project, Ralph Bierman and his associates demonstrated the living benefits of **IPS**-based self-help and community support programs throughout Canada. The project involved:

- Community leaders,
- Professional helpers,
- Parents,
- Professional teachers,
- Children.

Basically, the project demonstrated that community citizens could be trained in **IPS**-based skills to, first, help themselves and, second, help others, including especially their children.

Learning

Intervention designs for learning include:

- The "humanizing education" movement,
- The "psychological education" movement,
- The "lead teacher" movement,
- The relating model of discipline movement,
- The "learning-to-learn" movement,
- *"The Possibilities Teacher"* movement.

For example, David Aspy, Flora Roebuck, and associates conducted the first *"Possibilities Teacher"* projects as part of their **National Consortium for Humanizing Education.** They empowered tens of thousands of educators and children in **IPS** skills in more than 40 states and several foreign countries. This project involved:

- Principals,
- Teachers,
- Learners.

They found that the learners of trained teachers thrived while those of teachers who were not trained "plateaued" or deteriorated in scholastic and other kinds of performance.

Working

Intervention designs for working include:

- The career development movement,
- The career placement movement,
- The "worker preparation" movement,
- The **IPS**-based management movement,
- The "Relating Up, Down, and Sideways" supervisory movement,
- *"The Possibilities Worker"* movement.

For example, in the first comprehensive demonstration of *"The Possibilities Worker,"* John Kelly and his associates in IBM's *"Office of the*

Future" produced improved productivity benefits of **IPS**-based training with the following populations:

- Supervisors and managers,
- Data managers,
- Word processors.

The project was so successful that the managers wanted to claim "ownership" due to their *"uniquely personalized management styles."*

The most comprehensive demonstration of the role of relating skills in the development of living, learning, and working skills was conducted by William Anthony, Mikal Cohen, and their associates in psychiatric rehabilitation. The researchers demonstrated positive outcomes with all elements of residential, educational, vocational, and community support systems as well as lobbying and legislative systems. Working in all 50 states and consulting throughout the world, they present their own relating-driven image of a futuristic mental health system:

A Vision for the Mental Health System for the Millennium

1. A mental health system in which people with psychiatric disabilities are viewed holistically as people with positive attributes, and treated accordingly.

2. A mental health system committed to improving the residential, vocational, educational, and/or social status of each individual.

3. A mental health system in which people with psychiatric disabilities play a major role in planning and implementing the new system.

4. A mental health system that understands the importance of practitioners skilled in the technologies needed to achieve the processes and outcomes of psychiatric rehabilitation.

5. A mental health system guided by the vision of recovery.

(Anthony, Cohen, Farkas, and Gagne, 2002, p. 319)

Anthony himself summarized the implications of the effects of the relating skills orientation and the *"training as treatment"* approach to living, learning, and working skills application. Doing frequency tabulations of the word *"skill"* in the helping literature, he found no references prior to Carkhuff's 1974 keynote address to the American Personnel and Guidance Association. Subsequent to the address, the literature was replete with references to relating skills and living, learning, and working skills training as a *"preferred model of treatment."* The relating skills movement specifically and the life skills movement generically have changed the orientation to helping dramatically. Relating skills have helped make helping and teaching and managing productive professions. Their influence remains profound in all areas of human endeavor. They are the gifts of Carkhuff and Berenson: the necessary skills of human possibilities.

Summary and Transition

We may transition into the extraordinary extension of work by Carkhuff and Berenson by reporting their summation of research on the effects of **IPS** (Carkhuff, 1983):

> In summary, **IPS** are critical human ingredients because they facilitate the accomplishment of human goals. **IPS** help people to explore each others' frames of reference. **IPS** help people to understand the objectives for the tasks at hand. Finally, **IPS** help people to act upon their shared objectives. In short, **IPS** facilitate the focusing of human efforts.

> **IPS** help us to live more effectively with our families at home and to help more effectively our counselees in our counseling centers. **IPS** help us to teach and learn more effectively in our schools and training centers. **IPS** help us to work more effectively at our individual stations and in our organizations at work. In short, **IPS** facilitate our human productivity.

Overall, we stand about a 95% chance of accomplishing any human purposes when we have introduced interpersonal skills at high levels. Whether we train helpers or teachers or employers or their recipients in **IPS**, we accomplish our objectives far beyond the probabilities of chance. Conversely, when we do not introduce **IPS** at high levels, we stand a random chance of succeeding in any human endeavor. In conclusion, human productivity is in part a function of people's abilities to process interpersonally. Interpersonally skilled people, understanding each other accurately, can succeed at any reasonable human endeavor (p. 99).

With this early work, Carkhuff and Berenson established a platform upon which they built all of their other relating applications and transfers:

- *Possibilities Information,* or **Information Capital Development;**

- *Possibilities People,* or **Human Capital Development;**

- *Possibilities Organizations,* or **Organizational Capital Development;**

- *Possibilities Marketplaces,* or **Marketplace Capital Development;**

- *Possibilities Communities,* or **Community Capital Development;**

- *Possibilities Governance,* or **Governance Capital Development;**

- *Possibilities Economics,* or **Economic Capital Development;**

- *Possibilities Culture,* or **Cultural Capital Development.**

These are topics that will be explored in subsequent chapters. Together, they establish the prepotency of relating as the core of all human experience and the preconditions of all human possibilities.

References

Anthony, W. A. *Principles of Psychiatric Rehabilitation.* Baltimore: University Park Press, 1979.

Anthony, W. A., Cohen, M., Farkas, M., and Gagne, C. *Psychiatric Rehabilitation.* Boston: Boston University, 2002.

Aspy, D. N. and Roebuck, F. N. *Kids Don't Learn From People They Don't Like.* Amherst, MA: HRD Press, 1978.

Berenson, B. G. and Carkhuff, R. R. *Sources of Gain in Counseling and Psychotherapy.* New York: Holt, Rinehart & Winston, 1967.

Bierman, R. *Toward Meeting Fundamental Human Service Needs.* Guelph, Ontario: Human Service Community, Inc., 1976.

Carkhuff, R. R. *Helping and Human Relations. Volume I. Selection and Training.* New York: Holt, Rinehart & Winston, 1969.

Carkhuff, R. R. *Helping and Human Relations. Volume II. Practice and Research.* New York: Holt, Rinehart & Winston, 1969.

Carkhuff, R. R. *The Development of Human Resources.* New York: Holt, Rinehart & Winston, 1971.

Carkhuff, R. R. *The Art of Helping.* Amherst, MA: HRD Press, 1972.

Carkhuff, R. R. *IPS – Interpersonal Skills and Human Productivity.* Amherst, MA: HRD Press, 1983.

Carkhuff, R. R. and Berenson, B. G. *Beyond Counseling and Therapy.* New York: Holt, Rinehart & Winston, 1967.

Carkhuff, R. R. and Berenson, B. G. *Teaching as Treatment.* Amherst, MA: HRD Press, 1976.

Friel, T. W. *Educational and Career Exploration System. The Development of a Systematic, Computer-Based, Career Guidance Program.* New York: IBM, Inc., 1972.

Kelly, J. T. *The Effects of IPS Training Upon Word Processing Output in the Office of the Future.* New York: IBM, Inc., 1983.

Truax, C. B. and Carkhuff, R. R. *Toward Effective Counseling and Psychotherapy.* Chicago: Aldine, 1967.

3. The Possibilities Information

by Donald M. Benoit, M.Ed.
James Barnet, M.A.
Warren Epstein, M.A.
Gerald Oliver, D.Sc.

The Possibilities Information

MEANING

"Information" is the product of free, generative, thinking people.

Our methods for representing information are our tools for generating and communicating our ideation. Skilled information modeling—in the form of sentences, systems and schematics—enables us, frees us, to represent our ideas.

This chapter presents a uniquely powerful explanation of information modeling and its profound value in freeing people to actualize their ideational contributions to society.

For Carkhuff and Berenson, science is about developing information capital. Indeed, science itself is **Information Capital Development,** or **ICD:**

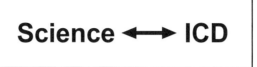

To understand this, we must understand what information is. We must also be perfectly clear on what it *is not:* information *is not* the concepts produced by connecting two or more data points. In this respect, the revolution in information technology presents a distinctive irony. Although it has succeeded in accomplishing many functions—above all, getting the right data to the right people at the right time—it has failed to define one critical component in its system: information!

For Carkhuff and Berenson, information is the relationship between phenomena and the representation of phenomena. Information may be represented at five different levels:

- **Conceptual information** that takes the form of verbal communications such as sentences;

- **Operational information** that takes the form of systems designs and matrices;

- **Dimensional information** that takes the form of schematic designs and model-building;

- **Vectorial information** that takes the form of vectorial models with force and direction;

- **Phenomenal information** that takes the form of phenomenal schematics that are asymmetrically curvilinear and changeable.

For our purposes, we are going to concentrate upon dimensional information in the form of model-building. Dimensional information is the next phase in science and an essential component of **ICD.** Later in this chapter, we shall present two examples of how *The Possibilities Schools* apply **ICD** in that most important of "laboratories": the classroom.

Dimensional Information: Model-Building

For Carkhuff and Berenson, model-building is dimensionalizing and, as such, it begins with scaling. In this context, scaling is an act of *generativity*. This means that the very act of scaling involves generative processing: generating new responses that are more productive than the existing responses. Of course, generative processing requires knowledge in one's substantive specialty.

Scales that accurately reflect our substance enable us to build models of phenomena. We may illustrate this principle with a scale for representing the levels of model-building (Table 3-1):

- Non-dimensional conceptual,
- One-dimensional linear scales,
- Two-dimensional matrices composed of scales,
- Three-dimensional models composed of matrices,
- Multidimensional models composed of 3D models.

Armed with dimensionalizing skills and substantive knowledge, we may define models for any phenomena.

Table 3-1. Levels of Model Building

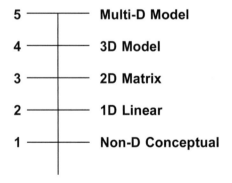

5	**Multi-D Model**
4	**3D Model**
3	**2D Matrix**
2	**1D Linear**
1	**Non-D Conceptual**

Non-D Conceptual

At the lowest level of model-building, people communicate information conceptually. The communications are usually in sentence form and have no dimensionality. When used inclusively, they do, however, cover the basic characteristics of the phenomena involved.

The most common of communications cover the basic interrogatives:

- **Who** is involved?
- **What** are they doing?
- **Why** are they doing it?
- **When** are they doing it?
- **Where** are they doing it?
- **How** are they doing it?
- **How well** are they doing it?

We label these basic interrogatives *"5W2H."* **5W2H** ensures the inclusiveness of all relevant characteristics of phenomena. It enables us to communicate definitions of objectives and to mobilize our resources to achieve these objectives. It does not, however, enable us to discriminate the relationships within, between, and among dimensions—relationships that operationally define phenomena. Operational definitions require scaling and dimensionalizing.

1D Linear

Scaling begins with one-dimensional, linear scales. These 1D scales make all other model-building possible. With scales accurately reflecting characteristics of the phenomena, powerful permutations and combinations of knowledge may be derived from model-building. Needless to say, without accurate scales, nothing is possible: indeed, inaccurate scales become *"depressor variables"* because they deceive us and mislead us.

Linear scales simply reflect the extremes of the phenomena we are addressing (see Table 3-2). As may be noted, scales are usually represented from low levels to high levels of some attribute of the phenomena. For example, if we were to scale relating (discussed in Chapter 2), our scales would range from non-attentive behaviors to highly personalized and initiative behaviors. Similarly, our model-building scales range from non-D to multidimensional modeling.

Table 3-2. One-Dimensional Linear Scales

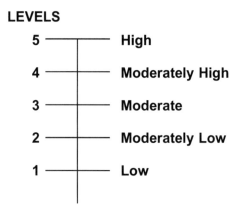

In scaling, a range of levels are positioned between the extremes of high and low; e.g., moderate, moderately high, moderately low. For example, in our scales for relating, attending would be preliminary to responding, with the latter a precondition for personalizing. Similarly, in model-building, 2D and 3D levels precede multidimensional levels.

Carkhuff and Berenson conclude that most people scale phenomena implicitly, not explicitly. For example, when people employ **5W2H** basic interrogatives in conceptualizing, they may be using implied scales (see Table 3-3). Note that here the conceptualizing levels range from facts to objectives, with the range defined by the basic interrogatives as follows:

- **Facts** – **Who** and **What** are involved?
- **Concepts** – **What** are they doing and to **Whom?**
- **Principles** – **Why** and **How** are they doing it?
- **Applications** – **Where** and **When** are they doing it?
- **Objectives** – **How Well** are they doing it?

These levels cover the range of conceptualizing skills defined by the basic interrogatives.

Table 3-3. Conceptualizing Scales

LEVELS OF CONCEPTUALIZING	DEFINING INTERROGATIVES
5. Objectives	How Well?
4. Applications	Where and When?
3. Principles	Why and How?
2. Concepts	What to Whom?
1. Facts	Who and What?

In possibilities scaling, all of the levels have the following characteristics:

- The levels are developmental and cumulative as they range from low to high.

- The levels of the phenomena that they describe are defined in processing terms.

- The levels and, thus, the phenomena are redefined from moment to moment as they are processed.

These characteristics enable the changes that take place with processing. In this context, the function of possibilities scaling is to enable us to enter phenomenal experiences; also to change along with these experiences as we become more intimate in processing them. Moreover, possibilities scaling enables us to develop models that accurately reflect the changing requirements of their environments.

2D Matrices

Carkhuff and Berenson find the magical effects of scaling in relating scales. For them, interrelating scales generates a whole series of interactions that we may not have addressed.

Matrices (or systems) interrelate the levels of two dimensions as shown in Figure 3-1. As we may see, every level of each dimension relates to every level of the other dimension. This enables us to address the interactions of all levels of all dimensions. For example, we may study the effects of high levels of one dimension upon low-to-high levels of another dimension and vice versa.

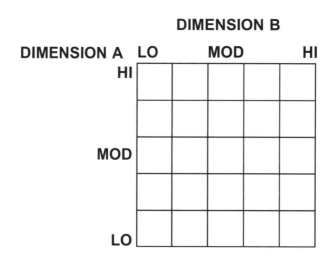

Figure 3-1. Two-Dimensional Matrix

Carkhuff and Berenson illustrate with their *Conceptualization Matrix*, shown in Figure 3-2. Here the levels of conceptualization have been inter-related with the basic interrogatives. Note that potentially every level of interrogative relates to every level of conceptualization. However, because the scales are developmental and cumulative, only the level of objectives is defined by all interrogatives: *Who? What? Why? When? Where? How? How Well?* Again, the levels are changeable with our processing.

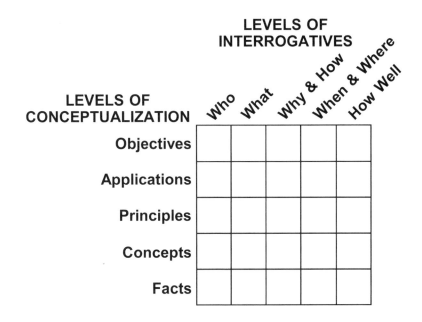

Figure 3-2. The Conceptualization Matrix

Carkhuff and Berenson offer still another two-dimensional image in the systems image shown in Figure 3-3. Here they have positioned the basic interrogatives in systems operations:

- **Resource Inputs**—**Who** and **What** are involved?
- **Results Outputs**—**What** is being done to **Whom?**
- **Transforming Processes**—**Why** and **How** are they doing it?
- **Contextual Conditions**—**When** and **Where** are they doing it?
- **Performance Standards**—**How Well** are they doing it?

Note that aligning the interrogatives in a systems design enables us to view the critical operations:

- **Results** that we are attempting to achieve,
- **Resources** that we are willing to invest,
- **Processes** that we are utilizing to transform the resources into results,
- **Conditions** that impose requirements upon us,
- **Standards** that we employ to assess our performance.

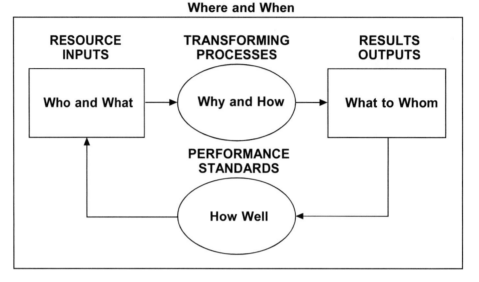

Figure 3-3. Systems Operations

3D Models

The generative effects become still more powerful as these scientists relate scales in three-dimensional models. Models or schematics interrelate the levels of three dimensions, as we may see in Figure 3-4. Notice that every level of each dimension relates to every level of every other dimension. Again, this enables us to address the interactions of all levels of all dimensions.

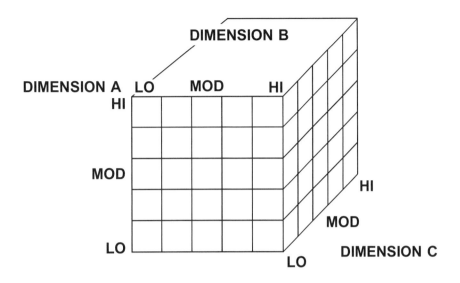

Figure 3-4. Three-Dimensional Modeling

In still another illustration, Carkhuff and Berenson interrelate the differentiated levels of operations (Figure 3-5):

- **Functions,** or results outputs, as defined by **What** is being done to **Whom;**

- **Components,** or resource inputs, as defined by **Who** and **What** are involved;

- **Processes,** or transforming procedures, as defined by **Why** and **How.**

Again, every level of operation clearly relates to every other level of operation. We will see the effects of modeling most clearly in multidimensional modeling.

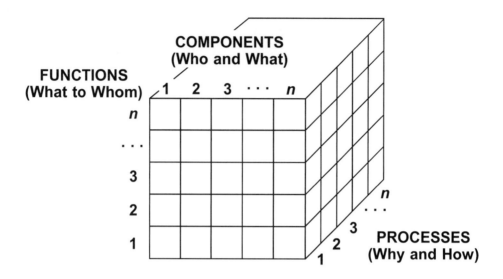

Figure 3-5. Modeling Operations

Multi-D Models

Carkhuff and Berenson empower us to view the generative effects of modeling in sharp relief in multidimensional modeling. We get to view the dimensionality of the conditions within which the phenomena are *"nested."* We also get to view the performance standards in their full dimensionality.

Multidimensional models interrelate the levels of many models, as shown in Figure 3-6. As may be noted, the phenomenal model *"nests,"* or exists within, the contextual conditions that are, themselves, defined dimensionally. Likewise, the phenomenal model generates its own performance standards, which are also defined dimensionally.

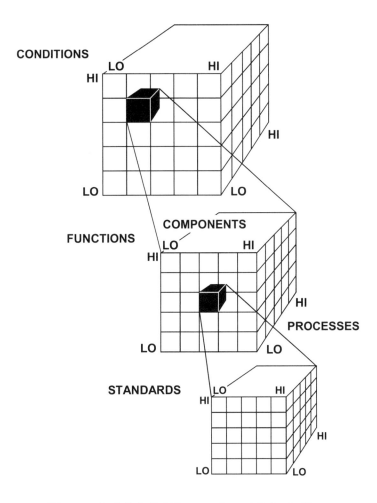

Figure 3-6. Multidimensional Modeling

In still another illustration, Carkhuff and Berenson interrelate the differential levels of all operations (Figure 3-7):

- **Functions** defined by **What** to **Whom;**
- **Components** defined by **Who** and **What;**
- **Processes** defined by **Why** and **How;**
- **Conditions** defined by **When** and **Where;**
- **Standards** defined by **How Well.**

Again, the levels interrelate. Also, the conditions and standards have their own dimensionality: functions, components, processes.

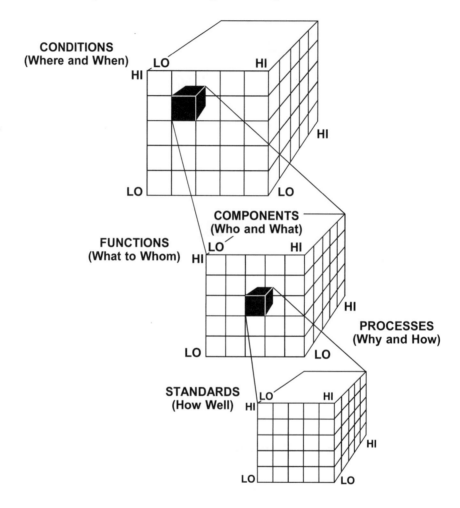

Figure 3-7. Multidimensional Modeling Operations

Applications in *The Possibilities Schools*

Now let us show you some examples of what goes on inside the classrooms of *The Possibilities Schools.*

The following is an illustration of applications of **5W2H** information in a sixth-grade English grammar class. It involves reasoning activities that will be presented in the next chapter, *"The Possibilities Humans,"* which focuses on human processing.

SENTENCES (5W2H)	ELEMENTARY SCHOOL GRAMMAR
	Elementary-school teacher is teaching basic grammar to sixth-grade students.
REPRESENTING	
WHO	**Student:** *Nouns* emphasize *who* is involved in acting.
WHAT	**Student:** And *objects* emphasize *what* is being accomplished by acting.
HOW	**Student:** *Verbs* tell us *how* they are acting.
WHY	**Student:** And *verbs* also tell us *why* they are acting.
WHERE & WHEN	**Student:** *Adverbs* tell us *where* and *when* they are acting.
HOW WELL	**Student:** *Adverbs* also tell us *how well* they are acting.
EXPANDING	
WHO ELSE	**Student:** *Nouns* also include *who else* and *what* are involved.

WHAT ELSE ▶

Student: *Objects* also emphasize *what* is being done to *whom.*

HOW & WHY ▶

Student: The same for the *verbs, how* and *why:* when we change the other parts, the procedures may change.

WHERE & WHEN ELSE ▶

Student: If the *nouns* and *verbs* change, the *adverbs* for *where* and *when* may change.

HOW WELL ▶

Student: If anything else changes, then our *adverbs* for measuring *how well* change.

NARROWING

WHO'S BEST ▶

Student: It's always best to include all the *nouns* — all the *whos* and *whats.*

WHAT'S BEST ▶

Student: The same thing for all the *objects* — *what* is being done to *whom.*

HOW & WHY'S BEST ▶

Student: And other *verbs* — especially *how* and *why.*

WHERE & WHEN'S BEST ▶

Student: The same for the *adverbs* for *where* and *when.*

HOW WELL ▶

Student: The same thing for the *adverbs* for *how well.*

SYSTEMS

GOAL ▶

Student: So let's put all the parts of speech together in a picture.

OPERATIONS

Student: I'll begin with the *nouns – who* and *what* are involved:

NOUNS

> Who
> &
> What

OPERATIONS

Student: Then there are the *objects – what* and *to whom* the action is being done:

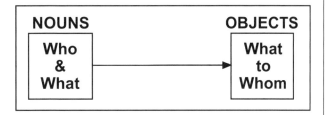

OPERATIONS

Student: Now we need the *verb* for explaining *why* and *how* it's being done:

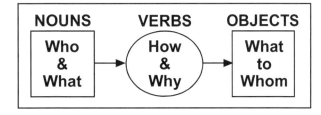

OPERATIONS

Student: All of this takes place in the context of modifying adverbs: *where* and *when*.

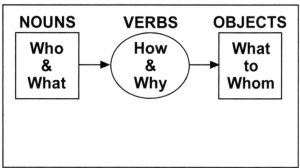

OPERATIONS

Student: All of this is modified with feedback from *how well* we performed.

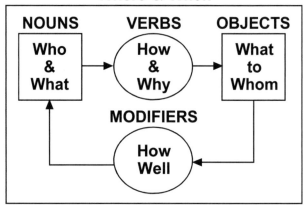

OPERATIONS

Student: Now we have a picture of how all the parts of speech relate.

SYSTEMS ▶ **Teacher:** It's called a system—where each operation is related to the other operations.

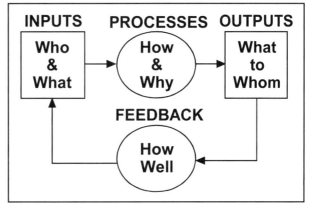

CONDITIONS
Where & When

INPUTS   PROCESSES   OUTPUTS

Who & What → How & Why → What to Whom

FEEDBACK

How Well

SYSTEMS ▶ **Student:** The system operates just like our parts of speech.

SYSTEMS ▶ **Teacher:** Grammar is a system. Indeed, it was the first human system.

PROGRAM ▶ **Student:** It should be easy to develop programs for other things like reading and writing.

PROGRAM ▶ **Teacher:** Let's try!

An extension of this application to writing compositions follows:

SENTENCES: **SIXTH-GRADE WRITING**

> **Elementary-school teacher is teaching basic writing skills to sixth-grade students.**

REPRESENTING

WHO ▶   **Student:**   We could begin by telling a story about *who*.

WHAT ▶   **Student:**   *What* is happening makes the story important.

HOW & WHY ▶   **Student:**   *How* and *why* it's happening explains the story.

WHERE & WHEN ▶   **Student:**   *Where* and *when* gives the story a context.

HOW WELL ▶   **Student:**   *How well* let's us know how successful the people have been.

EXPANDING

WHO ELSE ▶   **Student:**   *Who else* tells us the other people who might have been involved.

WHAT ELSE ▶   **Student:**   *What else* tells us other things they might have done.

HOW & WHY ELSE ▶   **Student:**   *How else* and *why else* gives us other possible explanations for things happening.

WHERE & WHEN ELSE ▶   **Student:**   *Where else* and *when else* change the conditions of the story.

HOW WELL ▶   **Student:**   *How well* gives us the changing importance of the story.

NARROWING

WHO'S BEST	**Student:** *Who's best* tells us the most important people to write about.
WHAT'S BEST	**Student:** *What's best* tells us the most important things they did.
HOW & WHY'S BEST	**Student:** *How's best* and *why's best* tells us the best way to explain things.
WHERE & WHEN'S BEST	**Student:** *Where's best* and *when's best* gives us the best conditions for the story.
HOW WELL	**Student:** *How well is best* let's us know the true importance of the story.

SYSTEMS

GOAL	**Student:** So let's put our writing program together.
OPERATIONS	**Student:** Our first paragraph could introduce *who* is involved and *what* they did.
OPERATIONS	**Student:** Then our second paragraph could tell us *how* and *why* they did it.
OPERATIONS	**Student:** So our third paragraph tells us *where* and *when* the story took place.
OPERATIONS	**Student:** And our fourth paragraph tells us *how well* they did.
OPERATIONS	**Student:** *How well* kind of summarizes the importance of the story.

SYSTEMS ▶ | **Student:** So let's summarize a picture of our writing system:

Paragraphs	Basic Questions
1	**Who** does **what** to **whom**
2	**How** and **why** they do it
3	**Where** and **when** they do it
4	**How well** they do it

PROGRAM ▶ | **Student:** Now all we need are some steps for writing each of these paragraphs.

Not only were the students able to learn grammar by **5W2H,** they were able to design their own writing system by **5W2H.**

Now here is an illustration of how processing **5W2H** in Social Studies can lead students to defining their own learning standards. This example also draws, in part, upon the human processing skills that we will learn about in the next chapter. It begins with a multiple-choice test in a middle-school class.

3. The Possibilities Information

MULTIPLE CHOICE: Select the correct response.

The primary reason that the South lost the Battle of Gettysburg was:

a. The North's superior positioning on Cemetery Ridge;

b. The South's lack of military intelligence regarding the North's positioning;

c. The South's inability to generate strategies to upset the North's advantages;

d. The South's total commitment to winning the battle-at-hand;

e. All of the above.

RELATING

GET

GIVE

GIVE

GIVE

Teacher:	We had some confusion about the answer to the multiple-choice question.
Student:	I thought the North's positioning by Buford framed the whole battle and that the South never got out of that box. So I answered *(a)*.
Student:	I believed the South lacked the military intelligence because Jeb Stuart was unavailable to Lee. I selected *(b)*.
Student:	Whether he was tired or not, Lee just couldn't bring himself to listen to Longstreet's outflanking strategies to turn the North from its positioning.

GIVE	**Student:**	I answered *(c)* too because Lee just kept calling for frontal attacks.
GIVE	**Student:**	I thought the big thing was that Lee kept focusing upon the battle as if it were the entire war. That's *(d)!*
MERGE	**Teacher:**	Maybe we're all saying the same thing: *"All of the above."*
MERGE	**Student:**	It seems like all of the answers are valid.
MERGE	**Student:**	It's a relief to know that there is not just one correct response.

REPRESENTING

SYSTEM	**Teacher:**	I'm confident that we can see all of these answers clearly in systems operations.
CONDITIONS	**Student:**	So the battlefield conditions were set by the North's positioning on the Ridge.
FUNCTIONS	**Student:**	And the functions outputs emphasized winning the battle.
COMPONENTS	**Student:**	And the component inputs lacked intelligence — they were fighting blind!
PROCESSES	**Student:**	And Lee's processes kept dictating frontal attacks.
STANDARDS	**Student:**	Standards were measured by this battle only.
SYSTEM	**Teacher:**	Let's put this together in our own comprehensive system of operations. [See Figure 3-8.]

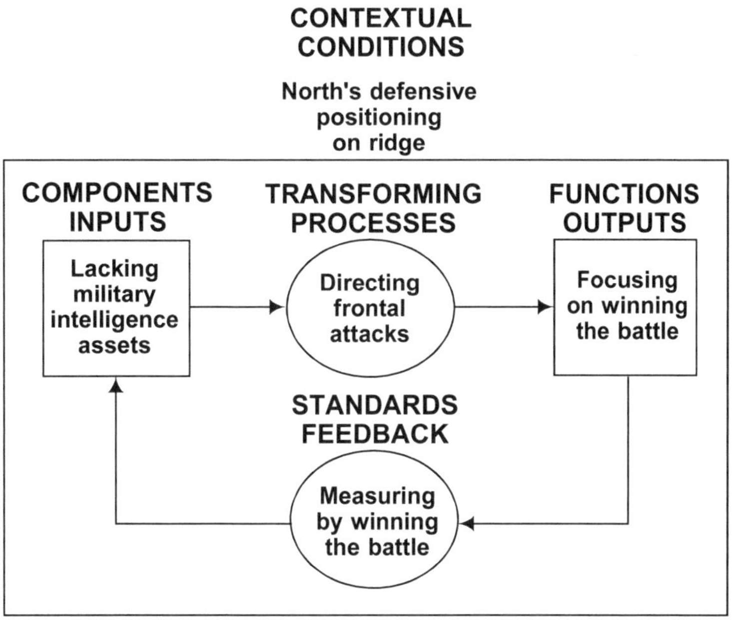

CONTEXTUAL CONDITIONS

North's defensive positioning on ridge

COMPONENTS INPUTS	TRANSFORMING PROCESSES	FUNCTIONS OUTPUTS
Lacking military intelligence assets	Directing frontal attacks	Focusing on winning the battle

STANDARDS FEEDBACK

Measuring by winning the battle

Figure 3-8. The South's System for Losing The Battle of Gettysburg

OPERATIONS

Students:	We can all see how all of these operations contributed to the South's loss.

REASONING

EXPANDING

Teacher:	Now how can we change this system to help Lee win the war?

FUNCTIONS

Student:	You already gave it away—you said the war is the function, not the battle.

CONDITIONS

Student:	We can turn the North's defensive positioning so that we don't have to fight in their box.

PROCESSES

Student: We can do this by enveloping them and causing them to withdraw.

COMPONENTS

Student: And develop new intelligence assets that enable them to ambush the withdrawing troops.

STANDARDS

Student: We can measure success by winning the greater war, rather than the battle.

SYSTEMS

Teacher: Let's see if we can view all of these winning operations in a systems representation. [See Figure 3-9.]

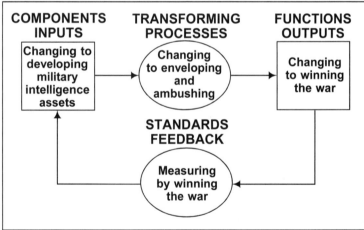

Figure 3-9. The South's System for Winning
The Battle of Gettysburg

OPERATIONS ▶ **Student:** I can see how you have to change your operations to win the war.

OPERATIONS ▶ **Student:** And expand your operations to pass the test!

NARROWING ▶ **Teacher:** Now let's narrow our focus to design a test that makes sense.

NARROWING ▶ **Student:** One we can all pass!

MULTIPLE CHOICES: Select the correct responses.

When General Lee was faced with the conditions of Gettysburg:

a. He should have turned the North's positioning by out-flanking from the right;
b. He should have focused on winning the war rather than a battle whose conditions were predetermined;
c. He should have focused on new territories where he could develop military intelligence assets;
d. He should have repositioned his main force to ambush the Northern troops as they withdrew toward the unprotected capital of Washington, D.C.;
e. All of the above.

NARROWING ▶ **Student:** I like that!

NARROWING ▶ **Student:** We can be test-makers instead of test-takers!

DOING ▶ **Teacher:** Why don't we try developing a system for test-making? [See Figure 3-10.]

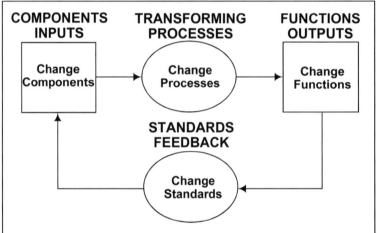

DOING | **Student:** All you have to do is change things!

DOING | **Students:** Change the functions!
Change the components!
Change the processes!
Change the conditions!
Change the standards!

**CONTEXTUAL
CONDITIONS**

Change Conditions

COMPONENTS INPUTS	TRANSFORMING PROCESSES	FUNCTIONS OUTPUTS
Change Components	Change Processes	Change Functions

**STANDARDS
FEEDBACK**

Change Standards

Figure 3-10. System for Making Tests

DOING | **Students:** Wow!

DOING | **Student:** We can take charge of our own learning.

DOING | **Student:** Our own tests!

DOING | **Teacher:** So let's develop our own test.

MULTIPLE CHOICES: Select the correct responses.

When test-makers develop testing items, they do the following:

a. Focus upon the function of memorizing the correct response;

b. Change the function slightly to elicit an incorrect response;

c. Change the components slightly to elicit another incorrect response;

d. Change the processes to elicit still another incorrect response;

e. All of the above.

DOING	**Students:**	Now we have a test for the teachers and test-makers!
DOING	**Student:**	Now we can control our own destinies!
DOING	**Student:**	Changing destinies!
DOING	**Teacher:**	And to think that we did all this by processing the Battle of Gettysburg!
DOING	**Student:**	*Thinking* is the right word!
DOING	**Student:**	History is just content!
DOING	**Student:**	It's static — unchanging!
DOING	**Student:**	This is truly a social science!
DOING	**Student:**	It's a process, not a content!

DOING	**Student:** It teaches us to process content.
DOING	**Student:** Content's output is process's input.
DOING	**Student:** We can process any content.
DOING	**Student:** And change it!
DOING	**Student:** And change ourselves!
DOING	**Student:** That's what possibilities thinking is all about!

Think about it! Students can generate their own informational images of their subject matter. They can control their own learning destinies. Can adults do less?!

For Carkhuff and Berenson, the impact of scaling is indeed magical! It enables us to develop multidimensional models to study the interactive effects of all dimensions. It also empowers us to generate whole new images of the phenomena.

The implications for human processing are profound. Indeed, without these representational images, systematic human processing is not possible: we cannot systematically generate new and more powerful images of phenomena without model-building. For Carkhuff and Berenson, it all begins with a simple scale that reflects our knowledge of substance.

References

Carkhuff, R. R. *Helping and Human Relations. Volume I. Selection and Training.* New York: Holt, Rinehart & Winston, 1969.

Carkhuff, R. R. *Helping and Human Relations. Volume II. Practice and Research.* New York: Holt, Rinehart & Winston, 1969.

Carkhuff, R. R., Benoit, D. M. and Griffin, A. H. *The New 3Rs: The Possibilities Teacher.* Amherst, MA: HRD Press, 2002.

Carkhuff, R. R., Benoit, D. M. and Griffin, A. H. *The Possibilities Schools Leader.* Amherst, MA: HRD Press, 2002.

Carkhuff, R. R. and Berenson, B. G. "Information Modeling—The New Scientific Components." Chapter 3 in *The New Science of Possibilities, Volume I.* Amherst, MA: HRD Press, 2000.

Carkhuff, R. R. and Berenson, B. G. "Information Representing Systems." Chapter 3 in *The Possibilities Leader.* Amherst, MA: HRD Press, 2000.

Carkhuff, R. R. and Berenson, B. G. "Managing Information Capital Development." Chapter 5 in *The Possibilities Organization.* Amherst, MA: HRD Press, 2000.

Carkhuff, R. R. and McCune, S. *The Possibilities Schools: A Blueprint for Education Capital in the 21st Century.* Amherst, MA: HRD Press, 2000.

4. The Possibilities Humans

by Debbi D. Anderson, D.Ed.
Irving Conrad, D.Ed.
Cindy Littlefield, M.A., C.A.G.S.
Susan Mackler, M.A., C.A.G.S.
Richard Muise, M.A., C.A.G.S.

The Possibilities Humans

MEANING

How do we define "essential skills of human performance?" What are their categories? What are their levels of performance? How do we measure them? We must ask and answer these questions to fulfill our growth and development responsibilities. At a minimum, we are responsible for our own performance. We may also have direct responsibilities for contributing to the growth and development of members of our extended families and communities. We all have some level of responsibility for understanding and elevating "human performance" within the social groups where we live, learn and work.

This chapter will orient us to a useful formula for human performance. We will find that the people who are most free score highest when measured against this formula for human performance while those least free rate lowest against these same measures.

It is said that great ideas often spring up simultaneously from different people in different places. This is the case of Jack Kilby and Robert Noyce, both of whom, in 1959, envisioned a semi-conductor — the microchip — that would change our worlds dramatically. It is also the case of Eli Ginzburg, Gary Becker, and Robert R. Carkhuff and Bernard G. Berenson in addressing human resource development **(HRD)** that would elevate our contributions to these changes.

In 1966, Eli Ginzburg addressed human resources in terms of *"manpower development and utilization"* in the private-sector organization.

In 1967, Gary Becker analyzed human capital as *"expenditures on people — for education, training, health — that in a broad sense raise productivity."*

In 1967, Carkhuff and Berenson defined individual human resource development as *"the creative and constructive outcomes of human relationships"* and in 1968, with Andrew H. Griffin, established the first **Center for Human Resource Development** at American International College in Springfield, Massachusetts.

For his contributions to organizational human resource development, Ginzburg received the acknowledgement of his business peers as *the father of human resources.*

For his contributions toward understanding *"capital expenditures,"* Becker received the recognition of his fellow economists and the **1992 Nobel Prize in Economics.**

For their contributions to individual human resource development, Carkhuff and Berenson received the opportunity to continue to do what they had always been doing: generative processing of the very nature of the models they were creating.

Carkhuff and Berenson generated new models and systems of human resources and, then, of human capital development, or **HCD** (see Table 4-1). They also analyzed the contributions of these models and systems to economic growth.

Table 4-1. Human Capital Development

LEVELS OF FUNCTIONING	PHYSICAL	EMOTIONAL		INTELLECTUAL				
	Physical Fitness	Personal Motivation	Interpersonal Relating	Information Relating	Information Representing	Individual Processing	Interpersonal Processing	Inter-dependent Processing
Leader	Stamina	Mission	Initiate	Objectives	Multi-D	Act	Go	Interdep. Acting
Contributor	Intensity	Actualize	Personalize	Applications	Nested D	Understand	Merge	Interdep. Understand
Participant	Adapt	Achieve	Respond	Principles	3D	Explore	Give	Interdep. Exploring
Observer	Survive	Incentive	Attend	Concepts	2D	Goal	Get	Interdep. Goaling
Detractor	Sick	Non-Incentive	Non-Attending	Facts	1D	Non-Preparation	Non-Engagement	Non-Engagement

As may be noted in Table 4-1, the scientists have defined the areas of **HCD:**

- Physical Fitness,
- Personal Motivation,
- Interpersonal Relating,
- Information Relating,
- Information Representing,
- Individual Processing,
- Interpersonal Processing,
- Interdependent Processing.

The scientists have also defined the levels of **HCD:**

- Leader,
- Contributor,
- Participant,
- Observer,
- Detractor.

The areas and levels operationally define **HCD.** For example, the *Participant Level* may be defined as follows:

- Physically Adaptive,
- Motivationally Achievement-Oriented,
- Interpersonally Responsive,
- Informationally Relating to Principles,
- Informationally Representing at 3D Level,
- Individually Exploring,
- Interpersonally Giving,
- Interdependently Exploring.

Together, the areas and levels of **HCD** yield diagnoses and prescriptions for training and empowerment.

Carkhuff and Berenson summarized the formula for **HCD** as follows:

$$\text{HCD} \leftrightarrow \text{P} \bullet \text{E}^2 \bullet \text{I}^5$$

As this formula makes clear, the power of **HCD** is in the intellectual processing.

First, these scientists seized upon the opportunity to generate models for individual **HRD** and converged them with the organizational and economic visions of **HRD.** Then, they transformed **HRD** into **HCD** by empowering and elevating intellectual processing systems. The following is a summary of their convergent conclusions, written by Carkhuff in 1983.

HRD: Converging Tracks

We can see the convergence of organizational and individual development most clearly in the goals for human resource development, or **HRD.** There are two distinct **HRD** tracks [Figure 4-1]. The first track, which we may call the organizational development track, grew out of work engineering before 1950. It emphasized developing human resources in order to increase business and industrial productivity. The second track grew out of the efforts of educators and counselors with a concern for human growth and development. We may term this track the individual development track. It placed its emphasis in education and human services upon developing human resources in order to actualize human potential.

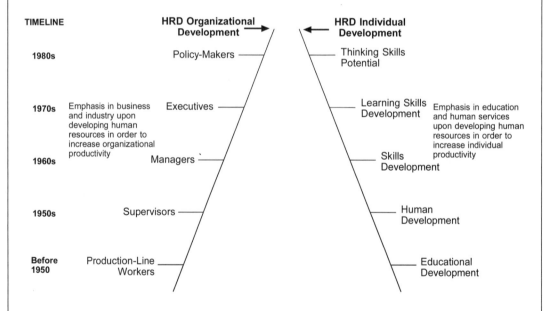

Figure 4-1. The Organizational and Individual Development Tracks of HRD

As can be seen in the figure, over a period of time the **HRD** organizational development track emphasized successively and cumulatively the development of human resources for all personnel involved in organizational development: production line workers or delivery personnel, supervisors, managers, executives, and policymakers. Similarly, over a period of time the **HRD** individual development track emphasized successively and cumulatively the development of all dimensions of individual human resources: educational, human, skills, learning development, and thinking skills.

As can also be seen, evolving from bases with totally divergent assumptions concerning organization and individual development, these tracks have evolved by successive approximations toward a common mission: actualizing individual performance and its contributions to organization productivity.

Beginning with a concern for the efficiency and effectiveness of organizational productivity of goods and services, the **HRD** organizational track has evolved toward a concern for individual productivity as a precondition of organizational productivity. Similarly, drawing from its concerns for the development and integrity of the individual, the **HRD** individual development systems have moved toward defining human resource development and organizational productivity as one and the same (Carkhuff, 1983, pp. 16–18).

It is also said that the great advances in human history have been made possible by reconciling apparently irreconcilable phenomena. For Carkhuff and Berenson, theory and practice converge in applied scientific hypothesis-testing. Indeed, civilization has moved forward through the efforts of a few who have integrated previously isolated positions. So it is with organizations, economics, and individuals. For Carkhuff and Berenson, all phenomena converge at the highest levels; it is their humble and scientific commitment to reach that level of perspective. It is in this context that they present their models for individual human processing as the prepotent ingredient of **HCD.**

The Human Processing Model

In this convergent context, the human processing model is based upon meeting the emerging requirements for thinking in the 21st century. It is derived from the processes of the possibilities science model:

- I^1 – Information relating,
- I^2 – Information representing,
- I^3 – Individual processing,
- I^4 – Interpersonal processing,
- I^5 – Interdependent processing.

In other words, human processing culminates in interdependent processing: interdependent processing with other human processors; interdependent processing with all phenomenal processing systems.

Processing Functions

For educational and empowering purposes, these levels of human processing were factored and scaled as *The New 3Rs* (Table 4-2):

- R^1 – Relating to information,
- R^2 – Representing information,
- R^3 – Reasoning with information.

These became the prepotent functions, or results outputs, of the human processing model. Succinctly, we relate to information in order to represent it; we represent information in order to reason with it. All other dimensions are dedicated to accomplishing these functions.

Table 4-2. Levels of Human Processing

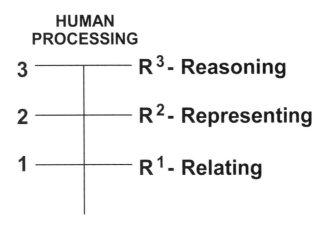

Information Components

Preeminent among the people, data, and thing resource inputs were the information components. Again, they were factored into *The New 3Ss* (Figure 4-2):

- S^1 — Sentence-driven interrogatives (1D information),
- S^2 — Systems-driven operations (2D information),
- S^3 — Schematics-driven systems (Multi-D information).

These become the prepotent components, or resource inputs, of the human processing model. Succinctly, the sentences are *nested* in systems that are *nested* in schematics such as modeling. As may be noted in the matrix that follows, these information inputs are dedicated to discharging human processing functions.

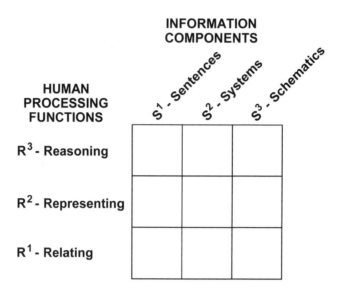

Figure 4-2. The Human Processing Matrix

Operational Processes

Dominant among all operations are the mechanical operations to which we have already been introduced (Figure 4-3):

- Functions, or results outputs;
- Components, or resource inputs;
- Processes, or transforming procedures.

These become the prepotent processes for transforming the resource inputs into results outputs. As may be noted in the human processing model, these transforming processes enable the information components to discharge the processing functions.

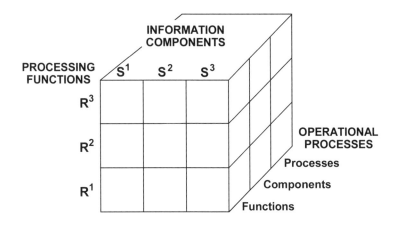

Figure 4-3. The Human Processing Model

Together, these dimensions define the human processing objectives:

Human processing functions are discharged by information components enabled by operational processes.

In turn, human processing defines human capital. It is precisely the capacity for generative processing that makes humans *"capital,"* or *"most important."* Moreover, it is precisely the capacity for generating new ideas for discharging organizational functions that makes humans *"capital"* in an organization.

The Organizational Processing Model

By rotating human processing inductively (clockwise) to become components, we may dedicate them to discharging organizational functions (Figure 4-4):

- Missions generated by leadership,
- Architecture designed by executives,
- Systems designed by managers,
- Objectives defined by supervisors,
- Tasks performed by delivery or production people.

These are the levels of functions inherited from the organizational processing systems.

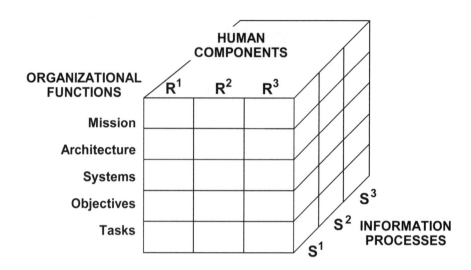

**Figure 4-4. Human Processing Components in
The Organizational Processing Model**

The human processing functions are rotated inductively to become components dedicated to discharging organizational functions:

- R^1 Relating,
- R^2 Representing,
- R^3 Reasoning.

The New 3Rs enable us to discharge all levels of organizational functions.

The information components are also rotated inductively to become enabling processes:

- S^1 Sentences,
- S^2 Systems,
- S^3 Schematics.

The New 3Ss enable *The New 3Rs* to discharge all levels of organizational functions. To understand fully how they do so, we must study the operations of *the human processing paradigm.*

The Human Processing Paradigm

We may view the phases of human processing operations in sharpest relief in the human processing paradigm (Figure 4-5). As we may see, the paradigm unfolds as a branching system or tree:

- **R^1 Relating**
  - Getting images
  - Giving images
  - Merging images

- **R^2 Representing**
  - S^1 Sentences
  - S^2 Systems
  - S^3 Schematics

- **R^3 Reasoning**
  - Expanding alternatives
  - Narrowing to preferred alternative
  - Doing by performing tasks to achieve objectives

Note that *The New 3Rs* are the critical phases in systematically generating new and more powerful responses:

- Relating by sharing and merging,
- Representing by operationalizing and dimensionalizing,
- Reasoning by expanding and narrowing alternatives.

To sum, we cannot reason without expanding and narrowing alternatives: we cannot expand and narrow without representing images; we cannot represent images without relating to information.

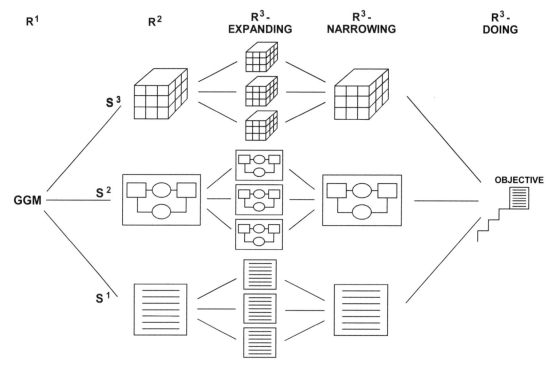

Figure 4-5. The Human Processing Paradigm

Possibilities Science

Perhaps the greatest product of the generative thinking of Carkhuff and Berenson is the new science itself. To generate this science, the researchers had to process their own generating processes:

- Relating to the scientific phenomena,
- Representing the scientific phenomena,
- Reasoning with the scientific phenomena.

The New Science of Possibilities is the product of their efforts: *the process is the product!*

The fundamental assumptions of probabilities science revolve around the principle of variability: variability is the range of deviations from some fixed and artificial central tendency such as a mean, median, or mode. The central tendency becomes the standard, and we seek to narrow our tolerances around the standard.

The fundamental assumptions of possibilities science revolve around the principle of changeability: changeability is the ongoing rotation of operations in the universe; these rotations enable the continuous interdependent processing of all phenomena.

Thus, the probabilities scientist seeks to continue some artificial ideal and to order everything and everyone in a way that conforms to that ideal. The science derives from this controlling function:

- We *describe* phenomenal operations.

- We *predict* phenomenal operations.

- We *control* phenomenal operations.

This controlling function has served humankind in the production of a spiraling array of goods and services. However, it does not align itself with the inherent changeability of all natural phenomena.

The possibilities scientist, while not abandoning probabilities science, seeks to align with the natural and changing rhythms of phenomena. Accordingly, the science culminates in a releasing or freeing function:

- We *relate* to phenomenal operations in order to understand their potential.

- We *empower* phenomenal operations in order to enhance their potential.

- We *free* phenomenal operations so they may actualize their potential.

This freeing function will serve humankind in the fulfillment of its potential and its environment's potential to actualize changeable destinies.

The central principle here is changeability. Changeability defines the standards by which we operationally define all phenomena:

FUNCTIONS	*Life-cycle processing functions are discharged*
COMPONENTS	*by unequal multidimensional modeling components*
PROCESSES	*enabled by interdependent phenomenal processing*
CONDITIONS	*under asymmetrically curvilinear environmental conditions*
STANDARDS	*with diversity and changeability standards.*

Changeability is thus the key to these operational definitions.

According to Carkhuff and Berenson, whereas variability seeks to fix phenomena statically, changeability seeks to align with, first, naturalistic operations and, second, empowering interventionistic effects upon these operations. Its view is inclusive, admitting variability as simply another instance of the changeable.

These two contrasting principles shape the core of two very different sciences. Probabilities science, which relies on variability, is highly artificial in origin, conceived by humankind to order and control its universe. This science fixes its data sources in linear data and thinking. In so doing, it loses most of the meaning of its measurements through so-called *"error variance."* In this context, chaos and even relativity are misinterpretations.

Possibilities science comes to us fashioned by observations of Nature itself. Nature speaks to us and tells us the following:

- All phenomena process.

- All phenomena are unequal in the power of their processing.

- All processing phenomena are nested in higher-order processing phenomena.

- All lower-order phenomena are genetically encoded by higher-order phenomena.

- All phenomena rotate to become drivers in processing (depending upon their purposes and ours).

Changeability is thus defined by all of these continuous operations:

- Phenomenal processing,
- Unequality of processing,
- Nested processing,
- Genetic encoding of processing,
- Rotating of processing systems.

Together, these operations make up the continuous interdependent processing systems that define changeability. If we are continuously and interdependently processing, then we are continuously changing.

Changeability is the prepotent construct. It generates an infinite array of spiraling standards and serves as the driving function for variability. Changeability and possibilities empower us to do *the right things,* while variability and probabilities enable us to do *things right.* On occasion, we may even dedicate changeability to variability and the eternal task of narrowing variability around static standards.

In short, changeability is the engine of possibilities — the energy source of Nature's intelligence. Variance may be employed to support a temporary commercial product or idea, or even scientific content; yet, all processing phenomena are ever, in truth, changeability companions.

We may continue with a summary from Carkhuff (1983) regarding the convergence of individual and organizational **HRD** in accomplishing the transformation of **HRD** into **HCD**.

HCD: Convergence

At the highest levels of productivity, the organizational and individual development tracks clearly converge: the previously separate actualization systems become one and the same [Figure 4-6]. The individual must be actualized in terms of his or her physical, emotional, and intellectual resources; living, learning, and working functions; and exploring, understanding, and acting processes. This actualization must occur within every function of the productivity system in order to actualize

---

productivity potential; i.e., policymaking and management as well as supervision and delivery. In a similar manner, the individual cannot actualize his or her potential without incorporating the skills of every function of the productivity system in every area of human endeavor: policy, executive, management, supervision, and delivery. These productivity system functions must be increasingly and cumulatively discharged at each developmental stage of the individual's actualization process. In other words, at the dependency stage, the individual can be productive only under the supervision of others; at the independence stage, the individual can manage and supervise his or her own productivity; and at the interdependency stage, the individual can develop his or her own policy and manage and supervise his or her own productivity, while teaching and learning with others and sharing in their databases.

In conclusion, it is clear that neither organizational nor individual actualization is possible without the other. Extraordinary gains in organizational productivity will take place only when all personnel have actualized their own individual potential. In the same context, no one person within an organization can actualize his or her potential until all persons in the organization have actualized their potentials. A deficit in one person's performance constitutes a non-actualizing experience for all other persons and thus detracts from their performance.

From a larger perspective, actualizing individual human potential is not possible without extraordinary organizational productivity. It is just such organizational productivity that frees the individual of the burdens of economic survival to fulfill the privileges of human growth. Indeed, as may be viewed in our figure, at the highest levels of productivity, organizational and individual actualization of **HCD** are one and the same: the actualization of human processing and productivity (Carkhuff, 1983, pp. 22–23).

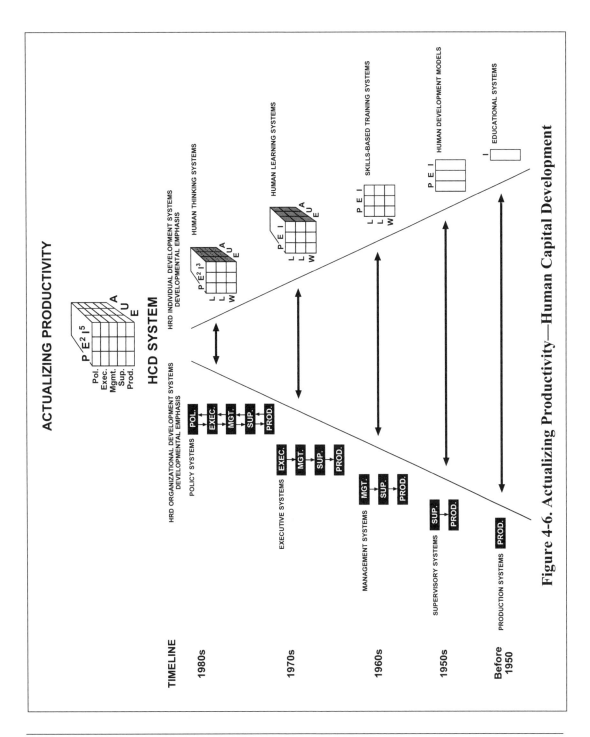

Figure 4-6. Actualizing Productivity—Human Capital Development

While Becker addressed the costs or *"capital expenditures"* of human capital, Carkhuff, Carnavale, and others have addressed the benefits that these costs have contributed. They partitioned variance in pursuing the sources of effect of economic productivity growth: human, information, and organizational capital development along with other forms of new capital. We conclude our review with Carkhuff's summary of nearly 20 years ago (Carkhuff, 1986).

Sources of Economic Growth

Historically, capital and natural resources accounted for the great majority of growth in productivity. Today, they account for a small minority of productivity growth. For example, in the first part of the century, capital and natural resources, including minerals, energy, and land, accounted for approximately 75% of our gross domestic product (GDP). Today, they account for much less.

Human and information resources are the great sources of productivity in the Information Age. Since the early 1900s, these resources have become increasingly dominant in relation to capital and natural resources. Improved quality and reconfiguration of labor through education, training, retraining, and "on-the-job know-how" have consistently accounted for the greatest amount of productivity improvement and growth in national income. In general, the higher the quality of human and information resources, the higher the growth in productivity.

When economists project the sources of economic growth, they conceive of factor or resource inputs and productivity components or organizational processing as the dominant sources. The resource input sources emphasize human and capital resources. The organizational processing sources include information resources or advancements in knowledge and human resources or, in their terms, skilled labor. In turn, the human resources are accounted for primarily by education and training and secondarily by health and workforce composition.

The moderate to high projections in national income range from 3.4% to 4.8%. The resource inputs account for between 1.8% and 2.2% of this growth. In turn, the organizational processing accounts for from 1.6% to 2.6% of the growth. In general, we may think of the input and processing component contributions as being approximately equal. However, the inputs decrease in contribution and the processing increases in contribution as the productivity growth projections increase. In other words, the higher the productivity growth, the greater is the influence of the organizational processing component.

Thus, we summarize the sources of projected economic growth (Figure 4-7). As can be seen, economic growth is accounted for by the resource inputs and organizational processing: the inputs and the processing each account for approximately 50% of the variability in projected economic growth.

$$\text{Economic Growth} = 50\% \text{ Resource Inputs} + 50\% \text{ Organizational Processing}$$

Figure 4-7. Equation for Economic Growth.

When we analyze the resource input components, we find that human resources account for the greatest percent of effect. In general, human resources account for around two-thirds, or 67%, of the input components, while capital resources account for around one-third, or 33%, of the input components. Other factors such as natural resources and land make negligible contributions.

It is important to understand that the human resource inputs to the organization system are outputs of other systems, particularly education and training, but also the home and community. Thus, the human resource inputs bring with them skills, knowledge, and attitudes based upon previous learning experiences. In other words, the current mode of analyzing resource inputs incorporates information resources within the human resources.

Thus, we represent the equation for resource inputs (Figure 4-8). For purposes of calculation, if we allocate the amount of variance ascribed to human resources equally to both human and information resources, we have an approximation of the relative impact of these factors: the human, information, and capital resources contribute about equally as resource inputs. It is important to keep in mind that the resource inputs, in total, contribute approximately 50% of the variance to overall economic growth. For our purposes, we may say that human, information, and capital resource inputs each contribute in the range of 15% to 20% of overall economic growth.

$$\text{Resource Inputs} = \text{33\% Human Resources} + \text{33\% Information Resources} + \text{33\% Capital Resources}$$

Figure 4-8. Equation for Resource Inputs

In turn, the organizational processing component breaks down to human and information resource factors (Figure 4-9). Advancements in knowledge, or "working smarter," account for around half of productivity growth. The quality of labor or personnel accounts for the other half, with the effects of some "depressor variables" subtracting from the net effects of knowledge and personnel quality. In addition, there is some tendency for the effects of information resources or knowledge to increase as the size of the growth projections increase. In other words, the more efficiently and effectively the personnel work, the greater the growth in productivity.

$$\text{Organizational Processing (HRD} \longleftrightarrow \text{IRD)} = \text{50\% Human Resource Development} + \text{50\% Information Resource Development}$$

Figure 4-9. Equation for Organizational Processing

4. The Possibilities Humans

In short, there is a relationship between human and information resources. As the skills of the human resources improve, the power of the information resources increases. Conversely, as the advancements in knowledge take place, the personnel are empowered. Together, human and information resources maintain a synergistic relationship where each contributes to the growth of the other and both contribute to the productivity growth of the organization.

Thus, we may represent the equation for organizational processing. As can be seen, human and information resources, alone and in interaction ($\leftrightarrow$) with each other, contribute equally to organizational processing. Again, for purposes of calculation, we may say that human and information resource processing components each contribute about 25% to overall economic growth.

In summary, we may postulate human and information resources as the prepotent sources of effect in economic growth (Figure 4-10). High-quality human and information resource inputs account for approximately 30% to 35% of overall economic growth. Human and information resource processing account for approximately 50% of overall economic growth. Together, human and information resources, alone as inputs and processes, and together in synergistic interaction with each other, account for 80% to 85% of projected economic growth in the Age of Information.

We represent an equation for the various sources of economic growth. As can be seen, the human, information, and capital resources contribute equally to the 50% of economic growth attributed to resource inputs. In addition, human and information resources, alone and in interaction with each other, account for the 50% of economic growth attributed to organizational processing. Again, we should remember that the greater the economic growth, the more potent a contributor is organizational processing (**HRD $\leftrightarrow$ IRD**). Indeed, we may conjecture that the more robust the organizational processing, the greater the economic growth.

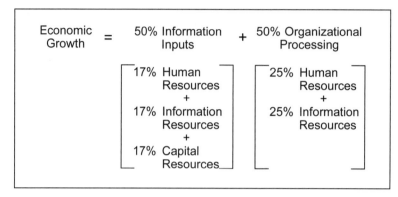

Figure 4-10. Equation for Sources of Economic Growth

Sources of Human and Information Resource Development

It is important to understand not only the ingredients of economic growth but also the sources of these ingredients. We must attempt to answer the critical questions: What are the sources of the human and information resource variables that account for 80% to 85% of projected economic growth? How can we impact human and information resource development to facilitate their contributions to economic growth? In other words, we may posit that individual and interpersonal processing account about equally for human and information resource development. It simply makes good sense that people process, first, independently and, then, simultaneously while processing interpersonally or interdependently with others.

From our own research, we have found interpersonal and individual skills each accounting for approximately 50% of the variability in the human and information processing **(HRD ↔ IRD)** which defines organizational processing. We represent our equation for human resource development (Figure 4-11). As can be seen, individual and interpersonal processing contribute about equally to the synergistic interaction of human and information resources that defines human and information resource development in organizational processing.

$$\text{Human Processing (HRD} \longleftrightarrow \text{IRD)} = \text{50\% Individual Processing} + \text{50\% Interpersonal Processing}$$

Figure 4-11. Equation for Human Processing

In addition, we may explore the relationship of education and training to human and information resource development. First, we may attribute the variability of human resource inputs to previous educational experiences in the home and in school. Second, we may explore data from the projections of the economists for the human and information resource development that occurs within the organizational processing component.

We represent the equation for human resource development within the organizational processing components (Figure 4-12). As can be seen, education and training account for approximately 80% of human resource development, while health and workforce composition each account for approximately 10%. For our purposes, of the overall economic growth, education and training account for the great majority of the effects of human resource development within the organizational processing component.

$$\text{Human Resource Development} = \text{80\% Education and Training} + \text{10\% Health} + \text{10\% Workforce Composition}$$

Figure 4-12. Equation for Human Resource Development

Thus, between human and information resource inputs and processing, we may conclude that education and training account for more than 50% of human and information resource development; 35% human and information resource inputs; and nearly all of the 25% of human resource development within the organizational processing component.

Finally, we may draw upon our research in other areas of human relations to understand the sources of training effectiveness. We have found that the most critical variables emphasize the trainer's level of functioning in the skills area being taught. Thus, the productive trainer is not only able to teach didactically, but most important, to model representatively the skills being taught. The remaining variance may be attributed to the development and organization of the content and the management of the learners' experiential exercising of the skills.

We may treat education and training in much the same manner as organizational productivity growth. In the instance of training, the training outputs focus upon the gain in trainee acquisition, application, and transfer of responses. Thus, training emphasizes transforming naive human resources into developed or skilled human resources.

We represent an equation for the effects of training (Figure 4-13). As can be seen, the critical sources of training are the training resource inputs and the training process itself. Our own research on the effects of training supports that trainers and trainees along with the content they are processing are the critical sources of effect — in the 80% to 85% range — in training gains. In this context, there is evidence to suggest that the prepotent source of effect is the discrepancy between the trainer's and the trainee's initial levels of functioning in the substantive area. In general, the trainees gain about one-half of the discrepancy between their levels of functioning and those of the trainers.

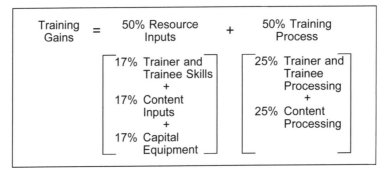

Figure 4-13. Equation for Effects of Training

Toward HCD ↔ ICD

What do these equations for human and information resource development sum to as the sources of economic growth? We may view the critical variables from a different perspective [see Figure 4-14]. As can be seen, education and training account for most of human processing, which, in turn, accounts for the vast majority of the human and information capital development **(HCD ↔ ICD)**. In turn, **HCD** and **ICD,** alone and in synergistic interaction, account for nearly all of economic productivity. In short, there is nearly a direct-line progression from education to economic growth.

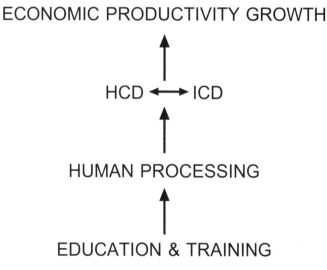

Figure 4-14. Sources of Human Processing

We may place the sources of human productivity in a still larger perspective [see Figure 4-15]. The interaction of education and the home may be seen as the source of human processing skills which account for human and information resource development **(HCD ↔ ICD).** In turn,

HCD and **ICD** are the primary sources of economic productivity growth and, thus, it is conjectured, human freedom. Together, economic productivity and freedom are the primary sources of peace and prosperity in our "global village."

As citizens of an increasingly smaller world, we may conjecture about the relationships of economic productivity and social and political freedom. The relationships may be reasoned logically by observing the differential in productivity in the free and totalitarian systems in the world. A few people simply cannot do the processing required of the many. In short, an empowered free people are a productive people and vice versa.

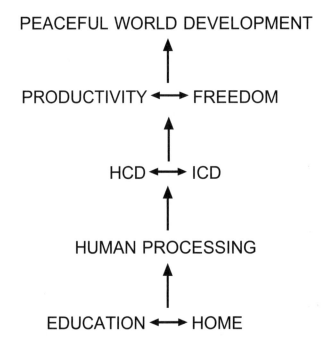

Figure 4-15. Sources of Human Productivity

This is not an ideological but rather a data-based debate. Most modern economic theories are, at best, irrelevant to today's human and information capital-based economies. In this context, it is important to respect — not revere — the past. Ninety-nine percent of the ideation in the history of humankind is occurring right now! It is difficult if not absurd to follow theorists who — however brilliant — had less than one percent of the data that is currently available.

Instead of traditional economic conditions, we can envision a succession of volcanic-like eruptions of scientific breakthroughs and innovative technologies, thus creating entirely new sources of economic growth. The entrepreneurial and intrapreneurial explosions that follow cannot be accounted for by traditional theories that account for less and less of the variance in economic growth.

The relationship between economic growth and employment growth is also a changing relationship. The expanding employment opportunities generated by the entrepreneurial organizations contrast vividly with the declining opportunities provided by large, established corporations. Transitionally, such relationships, typified by "Okun's law," are critical to healthy societies: unemployment declines as the economy expands beyond projected growth rates. However, with the extraordinary leverage of human processing, we must anticipate a time when economic productivity is so enormous that unemployment will not be of concern. Indeed, ultimately, we may envision the day when leisure will be the human mode and work may be a unique outlet for those seeking human fulfillment.

The precondition for this growth is human processing. The critical variables emphasize productive processing skills in interaction with the freedom to create. In this context, free enterprise in a free marketplace for organizations and nations is analogous to free choice for individuals.

The hope for prosperity and peace through productive world development lies in increasing both the freedom to create and the productivity to support this freedom: to make the pie large enough to empower the disenfranchised peoples of the world to become free and productive for their own purposes. All of this revolves around an evolving concept of human productivity. Economic productivity involves not only reducing resource investments while increasing results benefits. It emphasizes consumer productivity. Not only do we deliver products and services to consumers. We also deliver benefits. The core benefit is to help the consumers to become more productive at whatever it is they are about. Whether we are parents or teachers, business persons, government officials or community leaders, our business is to help our consumers stay in business. Consumer productivity is the guiding ethic of all human processing and, indeed, human endeavors.

At the other end of a human productivity delivery system, we must view the parenting—home, family, and community—that provides the human resources that are inputs to education. Currently, the home and family backgrounds account for most of the variance in the human resources exiting the secondary school systems in our country. In other words, learner pre-instructional variables relate very highly with learner post-instructional variables. However, when school personnel interact intensely with home, family, and community components, schools can elevate their ability to account for as much as 50% of the variability in learner resource development.

In summary, when each component of a human productivity delivery system brings itself into intimate and intense relations with the other components, then a systems synergy can produce exponentially more than the sum of the contributions of its components. Each part can impact every other part productively. Each healthy player can contribute more than his or her share through productive human processing. This human processing is the great source of human productivity. Indeed, this is the potentially infinite source of infinite human productivity leading to a productive, free, and peaceful world.

Toward Personal Growth

The pursuit of science is at once grand and enobling, yet highly problematic and humbling. It is an attempt to explicate the unknown—to make the unknown knowable. It is pursued through a mixture of data and research, of interpretation and meaning. Above all, its source is human experience, its gaps are filled by human intuition and are bridged by human conjecture.

There are no longer any laws of science—there never were! There are merely probabilities that serve to guide us to better or more productive possibility statements. These formulas for probabilities are pursued by people who are in part disinterested scholars and in part committed artists. They perpetuate the *"myth of probability."*

Even Einstein summarized blackboards and books full of data in an artistic equation for communicating a profound yet commercial formula for energy potential: $E = mc^2$. In a similar manner, all scientists—in fact, all people in the Age of Information, for all people are processors—must analyze, synthesize, and operationally define, and then creatively communicate, productive information.

All people—like scientists—must live their lives, learn their substance, work their jobs, fulfill their potential just as they test human experience: as tentative hypotheses to be supported or qualified or rejected according to the results of their testing, not in research, but in their momentary experience.

All people—like scientists—must be prepared to change their hypotheses and, thus, their lives with the results of their testing, for the Age of Information is, indeed, just that: an era of enormous information flow that comes to us from all points of our universes—internal as well as external—and at all times in our experience—sleeping as well as waking—human as well as extra-human.

In previous eras, people coined the expression, "the Man." There was, indeed, "the Man." He led the tribes of hunter-gatherers, directed the families of farmers, managed the assembly lines of industry. We even conceptualized the possibility of creating a new, computer-based "man," born of expert systems and reared in the artificial intelligence systems of the Electronics Era.

In the Information Age, information is "the Man." "The Man" brings its own meaning, carries its own ethics, dictates its own direction. We need only receive this information lovingly and process it systematically, and we will share in the excitement of birth and maturity, death and rebirth. As with the growth of productive information, we may grow forever.

It is certain that information is our life. To the extent we use our brains to process information, to that same extent do we ensure the building of potent, intense, and enduring neurons that define human life — for now and evermore. To the degree that we use information to empower people to make free and productive choices in their lives, to that same degree do we facilitate the movement of civilization into a great new **Age of Ideation** (Carkhuff, 1986, pp. 141–155).

References

Becker, G. S. *Human Capital and the Personal Distribution of Income.* Ann Arbor, Michigan: Institute of Public Administration, 1967.

Berenson, B. G. and Carkhuff, R. R. *Sources of Gain in Counseling and Psychotherapy.* New York: Holt, Rinehart & Winston, 1967.

Carkhuff, R. R. *Helping and Human Relations. Volume I. Selection and Training.* New York: Holt, Rinehart & Winston, 1969.

Carkhuff, R. R. *Helping and Human Relations. Volume II. Practice and Research.* New York: Holt, Rinehart & Winston, 1969.

Carkhuff, R. R. *The Development of Human Resources.* New York: Holt, Rinehart & Winston, 1971.

Carkhuff, R. R. *Sources of Human Productivity.* Amherst, MA: HRD Press, 1983.

Carkhuff, R. R. *The Exemplar.* Amherst, MA: HRD Press, 1984.

Carkhuff, R. R. *Human Processing and Human Productivity.* Amherst, MA: HRD Press, 1986.

Carkhuff, R. R. *Human Possibilities.* Amherst, MA: HRD Press, 2000.

Carkhuff, R. R. and Berenson, B. G. *Beyond Counseling and Therapy.* New York: Holt, Rinehart & Winston, 1967.

Carkhuff, R. R. and Berenson, B. G. *Human Capital Development. Volume I. HCD Models.* Amherst, MA: HRD Press, 2002.

Carkhuff, R. R. and Berenson, B. G. *Human Capital Development. Volume II. HCD Technologies.* Amherst, MA: HRD Press, 2002.

Carkhuff, R. R. and Berenson, B. G. *Possibilities Thinking.* Amherst, MA: HRD Press, 2002.

Carnavale, A. P. *Human Capital.* Washington, DC: American Society for Training and Development, 1983.

Ginzburg, E. *The Development of Human Resources.* New York: McGraw-Hill, 1966.

Wolfe, T. *Hooking Up!* New York: Farrar, Straus & Giroux, 2000.

5. The Possibilities Organization

by Christopher J. Carkhuff, M.A., Cert.
Rick Bellingham, Ph.D.
Warren Epstein, M.A.
T. W. Friel, Ph.D.
David C. Meyers, M.A.

The Possibilities Organization
MEANING

Organizations are vehicles for people to achieve things. Reciprocally, people are the vehicles that organizations employ to accomplish their missions. Indeed, how the resources of an organization are aligned define organizational effectiveness.

Organizations can stifle human performance or free people to contribute to their missions. Reciprocally, free, generative people define an organization's mission.

This chapter provides an operational view of an organizational architecture for aligning resources: marketplace positioning, the organization itself, people, information, and mechanical tools.

Attempting to anticipate future requirements in their marketplace, Companies A and B met for a series of discussions. These discussions between the two competitors centered on joint venturing to build the world's "cutting-edge" product. Utilizing the exact same market data, the companies positioned themselves differentially in the marketplace: Company A decided to continue on its current course and customize its standard product-line; Company B decided to "go it alone" in an attempt to tailor future product-lines to marketplace requirements. The implications of this differential positioning would be profound.

First of all, differential positioning in relation to the exact same market requirements means differences in values: differential positioning is a function of the interaction of values with requirements; power-positioning is an attempt to maximize meeting both values and requirements.

In this context, Company A's value system revolves around conservative, probabilistic principles: stick to what we do best and avoid taking risks.

In turn, Company B's value system revolves around progressive, possibilistic principles: reach for what we can do best and take the risks.

Moreover, both companies are differentiated in their corporate capacities, reflecting their values:

- *Company A is committed to maximizing the contributions of its powerful, existing technologies — mechanical and information technologies.*

- *Company B is committed to developing new corporate capacities to accomplish its initiative positioning — human, organizational, and marketplace technologies to drive its information and mechanical technologies.*

Their marketplace positioning established, the leaders of Company A spelled out a policy of incrementalism to deal with production bottlenecks and declining profits. The broad outlines of the plan included modernizing the computer systems, trimming thousands of jobs, and remaking relationships with the company's huge supply chain.

The redesign of assembly operations had already been underway for several years. However, at one point it got detoured by a big production push to compete with archrival, Company B. Company A won the competition, but the effort sent costs spiraling and profits down. In addition, global economic problems had an impact on Company A, leaving many orders unfilled.

However, Company A had a lot more going for it than met the eye on the profit sheet. It had historic positioning as the premier builder of products. Moreover, it had futuristic positioning as the exclusive builder of some products, for example, those from its defense division. Company A had also acquired companies that enabled it to have proprietary technologies, giving it a competitive edge in bidding on large defense contracts.

Company B, in turn, was positioned to become the standard-setter in the marketplace. This meant that it had to bring to bear not only "cutting-edge" mechanical and information technologies, but also "state-of-the-art" human, organizational, and marketplace technologies; moreover, it needed to integrate the applications of all of these technologies.

Here we have the extremes of marketplace positioning: one company dedicated historically to the customized variations of legacy learning; the other company dedicated futuristically to the potentially infinite variations of generative and innovative processing. Both compete on the same playing field: one with a conservative and stable game plan; the other with a continuous interdependent processing system dedicated to changing marketplace requirements.

The management of marketplace positioning projects the business and its enterprise networks in the marketplace. Positioning is futuristic in orientation. Managing marketplace positioning emphasizes preparing as-yet-unborn generations of business opportunities for continuous repositioning in the marketplace. We label the process of continuous marketplace positioning **"marketplace capital development,"** *or* **"MCD."**

Of course, many other forms of new capital development are directed by this positioning.

- *When the companies align operations with marketplace positioning, we say that they have developed* **organizational capital.**

- *When the people of both organizations are related and empowered to generate business innovations and solutions, we say that they have developed* **human capital.**

- *When the organizations incorporate new information-modeling technologies and concurrent planning for prototyping new designs, we say that they have developed* **information capital.**

- *Finally, when they incorporate new information-systems-driven mechanical technologies, such as "augmented reality" tools to track continuously changing wiring diagrams and parts lists, we say that they have developed* **mechanical capital.**

All forms of new capital development flow deductively from marketplace capital. The organizational capital is aligned with positioning. The human capital is empowered for implementation. The information capital is modeled to partner with humans in processing. The mechanical capital is partnered with information in tooling.

Positioned in the marketplace as an innovative standard-setter, Company B soon posed a problem to its people: they realized that their operations had reached a level of unmanageable complexity. To address this issue, they formed teams of exemplary engineers. Using the principles of concurrent engineering, they "factored out" all of the major operations of product building. They formed units representing major functions; then they factored within these major operations the primary functions upon which all unit components and processes had to bear.

In effect, the company formed a **"Team of Teams."** *Here is the approach the team used. Their mission was to develop* **Total Product Modeling.** *Their goals were as follows:*

1. *To implement global concurrent engineering,*

2. *To implement collaborative organizational processes,*

3. *To change their engineering processes from serial to parallel and, ultimately, to rapid prototyping – concurrent processing.*

Utilizing cross-functional analysis, the team of teams addressed the ingredients of their process-centric image: co-orchestrated organizational change to keep up with changes in the marketplace; cooperative organizational teaming methods (such as their demonstration of process reengineering); collaborative human-processing methods; communicative information technologies; and coordinated mechanical tooling, including information connectivity.

The team of teams believed they had an urgent need to technologize all of these areas in order to accomplish their mission of **Total Product Modeling.** *Their intent was to move upward from their current connectivity and communication to higher levels of objectives: collaboration, cooperation, and co-orchestration. It would be a movement toward possibilities organization.*

IP⁵D Development

The team of teams at Company B discovered the basic paradigm for possibilities organization and organizational change. Change is a function of **New Capital Development,** or **NCD,** systems (Figure 5-1):

- **MCD – Marketplace Capital Development,**
- **OCD – Organizational Capital Development,**
- **HCD – Human Capital Development,**
- **ICD – Information Capital Development,**
- **mCD – Mechanical Capital Development.**

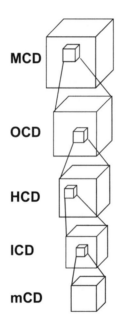

**Figure 5-1. The Possibilities Organization —
The New Capital Development System**

As we can see, each **NCD** system is *nested* in the marketplace system: **MCD > OCD > HCD > ICD > mCD. NCD** is the source of all organizational change. It made a difference for the team of teams at Company B, and can make a difference for us and our organizations too.

No matter how many customized versions of the standardized product-line, the planning paradigm "freezes" product design. Company A is stuck with the basic product it began with.

On the other hand, the processing paradigm "frees" the product to evolve in its most functional form. Company B has a spiraling, if not infinite, array of "virtual" products that can be tailored to specific customer requirements.

How did one company *box itself in* to an attenuating marketplace curve while the other company freed itself up to the growthful curve of marketplace commerciality? Clearly, one company drove by probabilities thinking or planning. The other company drove probabilities by possibilities thinking.

It was possibilities thinking that led the executives of Company B to relate to the phenomenon of putting out a product. They invited all potential contributors to this mission: customers, suppliers, vendors, and competitors as well as producers. They engaged these contributors in interdependent processing dedicated to an operational image of the product and a dimensional image of the processing operations leading to the product. In short, they engaged all contributors in a process of **IP⁵D.**

The story of **IP⁵D** is the story of how this possibilities vision was fleshed out. It is also the story of how 21ˢᵗ century corporations generate **NCD: MCD, OCD, HCD, ICD, mCD.** As such, it is a vital story for business in the future.

IP⁵D evolved from earlier forms of CAD/CAM definition:

- **EPD,** or Electronic Product Definition;

- **IPD,** or Integrated Process Definition.

Now **IP⁵D** develops and integrates all levels of processing.

For business purposes, we label our organizational design "**IP⁵D**" or **"Integrated Process Development."** It includes:

- **P⁵**, or positioning in the marketplace;
- **P⁴**, or partnering and aligning organizations;
- **P³**, or people or human processing;
- **P²**, or processing information models;
- **P¹**, or producing products or mechanical tools.

We can best understand **IP⁵D** by considering the role of new capital development, or **NCD,** in its development. This story of **OCD** is still unfolding.

The mission of the organization is **NCD:** the development and alignment of all **NCD** systems. The following sections describe the alignment of organizational responsibilities for **NCD.**

Aligning MCD

Those responsible for aligning the organization to support marketplace positioning must focus their efforts upon **MCD.** The model of marketplace capital development below (Figure 5-2) identifies the **MCD** functions, components, and processes.

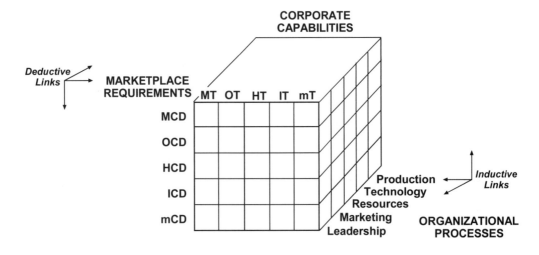

Figure 5-2. Marketplace Capital Development and Alignment

Let us take a closer look at the dimensions of the model:

- The **functions** of **MCD** are derived from the market's requirements for **NCD** systems: **MCD, OCD, HCD, ICD,** and **mCD.** Essentially, the marketplace of organizations is dedicated to fulfilling these **NCD** requirements.

- The **MCD components** are the corporate technologies available among organizations in the marketplace: **MT, OT, HT, IT, mT.** These technologies are critical to meeting the requirements of the marketplace.

- The **processes** of the **MCD** model are organizational processing systems: leadership, marketing, resources, technology, and production.

We can summarize these dimensions as follows:

Marketplace technologies are dedicated to new capital development enabled by organizational processing systems.

The relationships of these marketplace requirements, technological capabilities, and organizational processing systems define **MCD.** The interaction of these dimensions defines **MCD** alignment and the responsibilities of the **policy level** of the organization. Once we realize the interrelational nature of **MCD,** we may link these dimensions with intentionality, doing so deductively, inductively, or functionally.

Aligning OCD

Those responsible for aligning the organization to support organizational development and alignment must concentrate their efforts upon **OCD** (Figure 5-3).

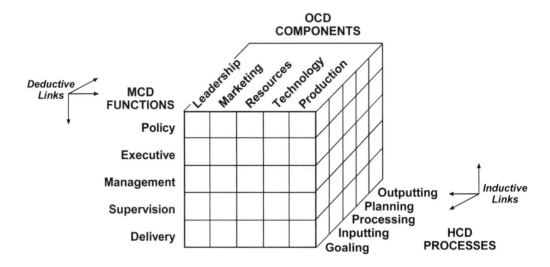

Figure 5-3. Organizational Capital Development and Alignment

Again, let us take a closer look at our model's dimensions:

- The **functions** of **OCD** are derived from the market's technology requirements. These requirements are translated operationally into functional levels of the organization: policy **(MT)**, executive **(OT)**, management **(HT)**, supervision **(IT)**, and delivery **(mT).** In other words, the resources of the organization will be dedicated to fulfilling these marketplace requirements.

- The **OCD components** are units of the organizations, and are derived from the processes of the **MCD** model: leadership, marketing, resources (and their integration), technology, and production. These organizational units are critical to fulfilling market requirements.

- The **processes** of the **OCD** model are introduced as HCD processes: goaling, inputting, processing, planning, and outputting. These processes are essential for fulfilling the organization's goals.

We can succinctly express these dimensions as follows:

> *OCD components are dedicated to MCD functions enabled by HCD processing systems.*

The relationship of **MCD** functions, **OCD** components, and **HCD** processes defines **OCD.** The interaction of these dimensions defines **OCD** alignment and the responsibilities of the **executive level** of the organization. Once we realize the interrelational nature of **OCD,** we may link its dimensions with intentionality, doing so deductively, inductively, or functionally.

Aligning HCD

Those responsible for aligning the organization to support the empowerment of human capital must focus upon **HCD** (Figure 5-4).

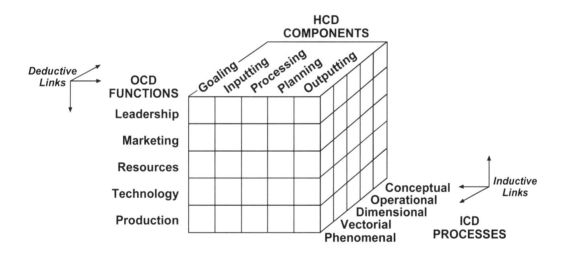

Figure 5-4. Human Capital Development and Alignment

We may note the following about our model's dimensions:

- **OCD** components have become the **HCD functions:** leadership, marketing, resources (and their integration), technology, and production. Essentially, human capital is dedicated to fulfilling these organizational goals.

- Similarly, the **HCD** processes of the **OCD** model have become the **HCD components:** goaling, inputting, processing, planning, and outputting. These human processing components are critical to fulfilling the goals of the organization.

- Finally, the **processes** of the **HCD** model are introduced as **ICD** processes: phenomenal, vectorial, dimensional, operational, and conceptual. These **ICD** processes are essential for human processing; they are the processes through which the **HCD** components discharge **OCD** functions.

We may also note that each lower-order ingredient is dedicated to enabling the achievement of a higher-order purpose:

> *HCD components are dedicated to OCD functions enabled by ICD processes.*

These relationships of **OCD** functions, **HCD** components, and **ICD** processes define **HCD.** The interaction of these dimensions defines **HCD** alignment and the responsibilities of the **management level** of the organization. Once we realize the interrelational nature of **HCD,** we may link its dimensions with intentionality, doing so deductively, inductively, or functionally.

Aligning ICD

Those responsible for aligning the organization to support information capital development must concentrate their efforts upon **ICD** (Figure 5-5).

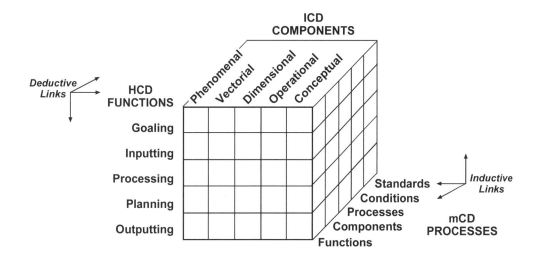

Figure 5-5. Information Capital Development and Alignment

We may note the following about our model's dimensions:

- The **functions** of **ICD** are derived from the **HCD** components: goaling, inputting, processing, planning, and outputting. Here, information capital is dedicated to service the requirements of thinking people.

- Likewise, the **ICD components** are derived from the **ICD** processes of the **HCD** model: phenomenal, vectorial, dimensional, operational, conceptual. These information components are critical ingredients in the service of human processing.

- Finally, the **processes** of the **ICD** model are introduced as **mCD** processes: functions, components, processes, conditions, and standards. These **mCD** operations enable the operationalizing processes and are essential to information capital processing.

Again, note that lower-order ingredients are dedicated to achieving higher-order purposes:

> *ICD components service HCD functions, or goals, through mCD processes.*

These interactions of **HCD** functions, **ICD** components, and **mCD** processes define **ICD** and its alignment and the responsibilities of the **supervisory level** of the organization. We may now link these dimensions with intentionality as well, deductively, inductively, or functionally.

Aligning mCD

Those responsible for aligning the organization to support mechanical capital development must focus their efforts upon **mCD** (Figure 5-6).

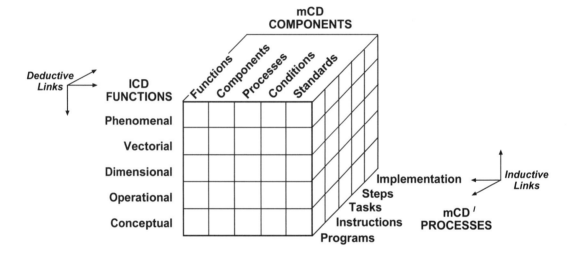

Figure 5-6. Mechanical Capital Development and Alignment

As we can see, the following describes our model's dimensions:

- The **ICD** components have become the **functions** of **mCD**: phenomenal, vectorial, dimensional, operational, and conceptual. Mechanical components, or tools, are dedicated to service information designs, or **ICD.**

- In turn, the **mCD** processes of the **ICD** model have become **mCD** **components:** functions, components, processes, conditions, and standards. These mechanical components are critical to fulfilling information designs.

- Finally, new **mCD'** programming **processes** are introduced: programs, instructions, tasks, steps, and implementation. These programmatic mechanical processes are essential to mechanical processing.

Once again, lower-order ingredients are dedicated to higher-order purposes:

> The **mCD** components service **ICD** functions through **mCD'** processes.

The interaction of these dimensions and their relationships define **mCD** and its alignment and the responsibilities of the **delivery level** of the organization. We may now also link these dimensions with intentionality, doing so deductively, inductively, or functionally.

In the **Possibilities Organization,** the dimensions of **NCD** are nested, encoded, and rotated according to the functions to which they are dedicated. This means that responsibilities within **MCD** are continuously changing:

- **OCD** within **MCD**;
- **HCD** within **OCD**;
- **ICD** within **HCD**;
- **mCD** within **ICD**.

All forms of **NCD** are responsibilities within **NCD**: **MCD, OCD, HCD, ICD, mCD.** The dimensions of the **NCD** marketplace universe are also continuously changing.

IP⁵D Applications

Historic probabilities science found its contributions in content-centricity or specificity: the linear, independent, symmetrical, and static. Current probabilities science finds its contributions in network-centricity: the ultimate distribution of the content discovered at its "nodes." Indeed, its adherents believe in the "truth" yielded by the Internet and other modes of distribution with the willing participation of content-centric scientists.

In contrast, possibilities science is futuristic, continuously discovering its changeable "truths" in process-centricity. All phenomenal dimensions are processing dimensions: functions, components, processes, conditions, standards. All processing is continuous within, between, and among all phenomenal dimensions: multidimensional, interdependent, asymmetrical, and changeable. At the highest levels of all phenomenal dimensions, phenomena are to seek their own changeable destinies.

All of the possibilities projects illustrated in this book have the quality of interdependent relatedness; thus, they have meaning. Demonstrations in the marketplace and the community, in business and organizations, with education and individuals, all derive from the same basic model of possibilities science. Moreover, these diverse projects are, themselves, held together by the changeable conditions of process-centricity.

A deeper look into the illustrations will reveal the organizational model dedicated to new capital development functions (see Figure 5-7); this is our **IP⁵D — Integrated Process Development** model. As shown, **IP⁵D** represents variations of the **NCD** theme.

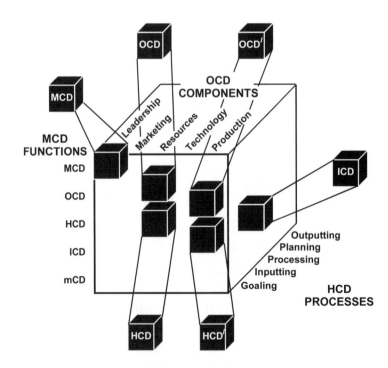

Figure 5-7. IP⁵D Model

For example, the following projects were mapped into the organizational functions, components, and processes.

 Corporate productivity upgrade as dedicated to **MCD:**
Marketplace-positioning functions are discharged by leadership-driven components enabled by goaling processes.

 Hybrid organizational modeling as dedicated to **OCD:**
Organizational alignment functions are discharged by marketing-driven components enabled by inputting processes.

 Internal organizational-alignment modeling as dedicated to **OCD':**
Internal organizational-alignment functions are discharged by resource-driven components enabled by generative processing.

 Internal team- and individual-performance alignment modeling as dedicated to **HCD:**
Internal human-processing alignment functions are discharged by marketing-driven components enabled by inputting processes.

 Possibilities processing systems as dedicated to **HCD':**
Human processing functions are discharged by resource-driven components enabled by generative processes.

 Concurrent processing systems as dedicated to **ICD:**
Information-modeling functions are discharged by resource-driven components enabled by generative processes.

We may summarize the overall **NCD** mission as:

MCD functions are discharged by OCD components enabled by HCD processes.

IP⁵D Virtual Representing

Paradigmetric modeling is dedicated to generating paradigms for both phenomena and their measurements. Indeed, the phenomena and their measurements are one and the same: the same scales that we generate for the phenomenal paradigms serve to measure the robustness of those paradigms. These scales generate *"possibilities objects"* for concurrent organizational modeling and process alignment.

One way to view paradigmetric modeling is as a horizontal assembly-line dedicated to developing solutions, products and services, or anything else. This view is represented in Figure 5-8. The process is initiated with ***The MCD Matrix:***

- ***MCD*** *marketplace-positioning functions are discharged by components representing corporate capacities in* ***MCD*** *technologies.*

The process continues with ***The OCD Matrix:***

- ***OCD*** *alignment functions are discharged by* ***HCD*** *human-processing components.*

Similarly, the process continues with ***The ICD Matrix:***

- ***HCD*** *processing functions are discharged by* ***ICD*** *information-modeling components.*

Finally, the process culminates with ***The mCD Matrix:***

- ***ICD****-modeling functions are discharged by* ***mCD*** *mechanical-tooling components.*

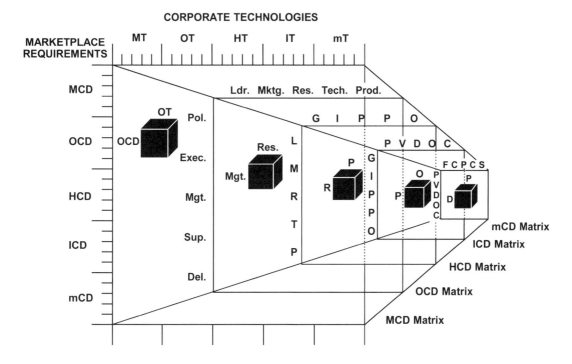

Figure 5-8. IP⁵D Virtual Representation

As shown above, each successive **NCD** matrix is *nested* within the previous matrix: **MCD > OCD > HCD > ICD > mCD.** This means that all of the processing occurs within the original **MCD** matrix; therefore, all of the processing objects are generated within *The MCD Matrix.*

As also shown, all of the objects are sized according to the matrices that nest them; thus the objects diminish in size from **MCD** to **mCD.** The first, or largest, nested object occurs within *The MCD Matrix:*

- *OCD organization-alignment functions are discharged by OCD corporate-technological capacities.*

In turn, the next-largest object occurs within *The OCD Matrix:*

- *Management systems functions are discharged by resource-integration components.*

Similarly, the next nested object occurs within *The HCD Matrix:*

- *Resource-integration functions are discharged by processing components.*

Likewise, the next object occurs within *The ICD Matrix:*

- *Planning functions are discharged by operationalizing components.*

Finally, the last, or smallest, nested object occurs within *The mCD Matrix:*

- *Dimensionalizing functions are discharged by processing components.*

Again, all interdependent common object models are *nested* within the original **MCD** matrix. We can employ paradigmetric modeling to generate any phenomena and their measurements.

Further IP⁵D Applications

A heuristic example for imaging paradigmetric technologies and their applications is "solid modeling." Just as computer programs that enable solid product modeling dramatically increased productivity in designing and manufacturing components, *"process modeling"* software will radically increase the productivity of the interrelated business processes of the extended enterprise.

The master matrix for process modeling is presented in the manufacturing illustration which follows (Figure 5-9). As we can see, the master matrix for manufacturing emphasizes market-player functions for involvement in constellation processing: producer, partners, suppliers, vendors, customers. In turn, the manufacturing processes are the components dedicated to discharging these market-player functions: feasibility, concept, definition, development, service. All other **NCD** systems are nested within this master manufacturing matrix: manufacturing processes discharging market-player processing functions.

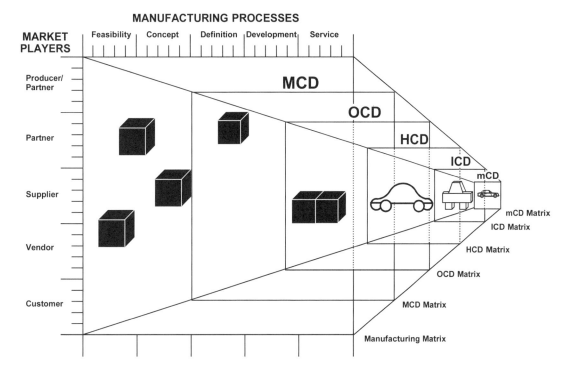

Figure 5-9. IP⁵D Applications

In this computer modeling context, all of the cells within the *"manufacturing matrix"* are interdependent *"common objects"*. The process modeling system moves through common object modeling of all the New Capital Development matrices to the production of products.

With paradigmetrics, we are empowered to fulfill the destiny of information technology: information modeling-driven manufacturing processes. Current organizational processing systems are out of sync, attempting to discharge **MCD** positioning functions with **mCD** tooling components. More powerful organizational processing systems will attempt to discharge **MCD** positioning functions with **ICD**-modeling components. Future organizational processing systems will bring **NCD** operations into more appropriate alignment: first, to become discharged by **HCD** processing; next, to become driven by **OCD** alignment; finally, to become driven by **MCD** positioning.

Of course, the rotations may be recursive: they may curve around to recycle iterations of rotations in a *"Perpetual-Motion Business Machine."* All that corporations require are the technological capacities of the paradigmetric tools of possibilities science so they can relate, empower, and free themselves to exponential and then potentially infinite corporate-productivity growth.

IP⁵D Implications

The implications for marketplace positioning are profound. As the global economy becomes integrated and interdependent, marketplace positioning likewise becomes interdependent and integrated. Financial capital continues to obey the basic laws of economics: financial resources are continuously invested and reinvested in the most valued uses. An interdependent global economy funds capital migrating freely to realize the best returns, thus making the economy more resilient. In short, market capital will "chase" the most powerfully positioned companies into the future, rather than allow them to fall into the past.

As explained earlier, managing marketplace positioning projects the business and its enterprise networks in the marketplace. Positioning is futuristic in orientation. Managing marketplace positioning emphasizes preparing as-yet-unborn generations of business opportunities for continuous repositioning in the marketplace. We label this process **MCD,** because it dictates the future success of our companies.

We can best understand the actual nature of positioning by considering its sources. Let us consider the sources of positioning for our two manufacturers: Company A and Company B. Both are positioned as manufacturing companies dedicated to delivering high-quality products at the lowest costs. Both are leaders in the industry, each with remarkable track records. Both are dedicated to market share for the business and profit share for their customers.

What makes these two companies different is their dedication to different paradigms. One company employs the probabilities paradigm that dominated the Industrial Age: *the continuous planning of operations to achieve fixed goals.* The other company uses the possibilities paradigm now emerging in the

Information Age: *the continuous processing of operations dedicated to continuous evolving goals.*

Company A is planning-centric within the probabilities paradigm. Once the goals are fixed, the planning systems emanate out to the various operations. Moreover, because the goals are fixed, the planning systems are driven by politically sensitive, internal negotiations leading to consensus among technical experts.

This planning-centric paradigm generates all of Company A's organizational functions:

- Marketplace positioning that is fixed;

- Organizational alignment that is politically negotiated with customer organizations as well as executives;

- Human performance that is directed by **S–O–R** discriminative learning or branching systems;

- Information modeling that is driven by **S–R** conditioned responding systems;

- Mechanical tooling that is implemented by **s–r** mechanical chaining systems.

Company B, in turn, is process-centric within the possibilities paradigm: the engineers process for and with the phenomena of the product in order to generate their most powerful images. The processing operations are focused upon the phenomena of the product. Moreover, because the images are continuously changing, the processing systems are substantive, not political: they emphasize the substance of the operations in a never-ending attempt to generate more powerful images of the product.

This process-centric paradigm generates all of Company B's organizational functions:

- Marketplace positioning that is continuously evolving and substantively driven by product-engineering principles;

- Organizational alignment that is continuously generated by concurrent process engineering;

- Human processing that is empowered to generate by **S–P–R** generative processing systems;

- Information modeling that is driven by **S–O–R** discriminative learning systems;

- Mechanical tooling that is implemented by **S–R** mechanical processing systems.

Indeed, companies A and B contrast vividly in the processing systems available to them to discharge organizational functions. Table 5-1, on the following page, illustrates this contrast:

- Company A does not even have processing systems for discharging organizational functions; it lacks …

  - **S–MP–R** marketplace processing systems,
  - **S–OP–R** organizational processing systems,
  - **S–P–R** human processing systems.

- The remainder of Company A's systems are slotted one level behind Company B's elevated processing systems.

Table 5-1. Comparative Processing Systems

	COMPANY A	COMPANY B
Marketplace Positioning	Fixed Marketplace Positioning	S–MP–R Marketplace Processing
Organizational Alignment	Politically Negotiated Organizational Alignment	S–OP–R Organizational Processing
Human Processing	S–O–R Discriminative Learning	S–P–R Generative Processing
Information Modeling	S–R Conditioned Responding	S–O–R Discriminative Learning
Mechanical Tooling	s–r Conditioning Chains	S–R Conditioned Responding

As a consequence, Company A brings the conditioning paradigm of the Industrial Age to the marketplace. After the goals are set and the plans are drawn, all of the assembly systems decompose into conditioned responding systems:

- Fixed marketplace positioning,
- Politically negotiated organizational alignment,
- **S–O–R** discriminative planning systems,
- **S–R** conditioned modeling systems,
- **s–r** conditioned-chaining tooling systems.

In turn, Company B emphasizes the evolving process-centric requirements of the Information Age:

- **S–MP–R** marketplace positioning systems,
- **S–OP–R** organizational alignment systems,
- **S–P–R** human processing systems,
- **S–O–R** discriminative modeling systems,
- **S–R** conditioned-responding tooling systems.

In short, Company B's process-centric paradigm generates new capital development:

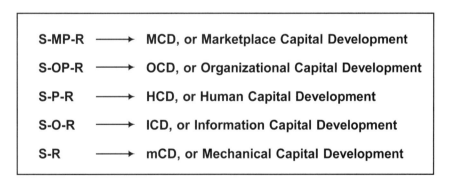

Of course, the best positionings in the market are those not yet taken:

- Partnered constellation positioning with producers, suppliers, and vendors to develop marketplace capital in the changing marketplace;

- Relationship-driven marketing that actually empowers customer organizations to develop organizational capital;

- Empowering human processing systems that actually empower people to process interdependently as human capital;

- Information modeling systems that actually yield information capital which can be processed synergistically with human capital;

- Mechanical tooling systems that implement information systems-driven mechanical capital.

These positionings truly differentiate the corporation or product in the marketplace. They empower the organization and its partners and customers with new capital development. They underscore that the most powerful positioning is substantive positioning: positioning that we can really deliver; positioning that we can follow through upon; positioning that we can build upon for ourselves and our friends.

The New Platform for the New Economy

Carkhuff and Berenson propose that there really is a new economy undergirding our economic growth. Indeed, the very reason that the recession has been shallow is the continuous elevation of **Economic Productivity Growth,** or **EPG.** The sources of this **EPG** are the most important considerations in developing the new platform for the new economy.

The meaning of the term *"capital"* notwithstanding, the new capital development, **NCD** ingredients are now the prepotent sources of economic productivity growth:

- **MCD,** or marketplace positioning;
- **OCD,** or organizational alignment;
- **HCD,** or human processing;
- **ICD,** or information modeling;
- **mCD,** or mechanical tooling.

Together, these **NCD** ingredients have displaced financial capital as the most important conditions of economic productivity growth. To be sure, financial capital remains a necessary catalyst to growth, accounting for somewhere in the range of 12% of **EPG.** However, for most purposes, financial capital development is a means of keeping score.

Together, these emerging **NCD** ingredients constitute a new and expanding universe within which the spaces and objects of **IP^{5}D** are integrated. Together, these emerging **NCD** ingredients constitute the explosive sources of spiraling economic growth. It is as if we are merely in the foothills of a volcanic and growing mountain range created by the global market, the Internet, and other new platforms of free enterprise.

The known **NCD** ingredients are integrated in **IP^{5}D** (see Figure 5-10). The emerging **NCD** ingredients will be integrated in **IP^{9}D** or **IP^{10}D** or some other exponential. Together, they will empower us to reposition ourselves continuously in our expanding universes, meeting and then generating changing requirements and capacities. This is the contribution of Carkhuff and Berenson to marketplace and organization possibilities and business possibilities generally.

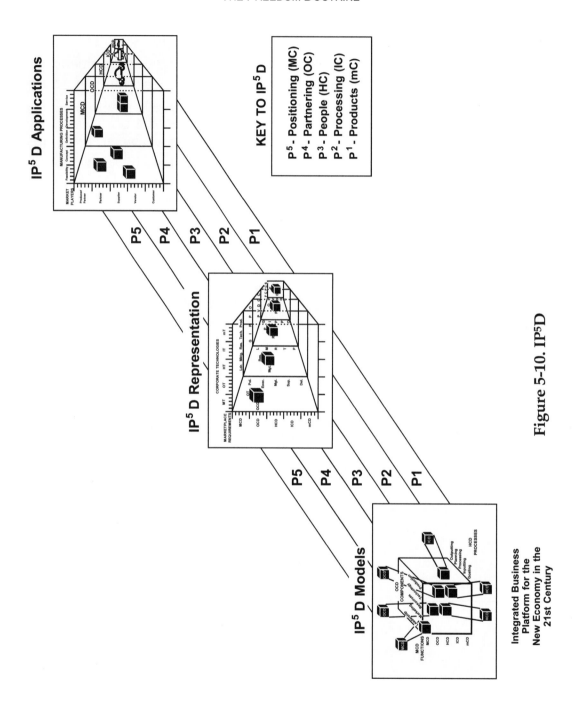

Figure 5-10. IP⁵D

References

Carkhuff, C. J. and Cook, A. A. *A Computerized HCD/OCD Collaborative Model.* McLean, VA: Carkhuff Thinking Systems, Inc., 2002.

Carkhuff, R. R. *Sources of Human Productivity.* Amherst, MA: HRD Press, 1983.

Carkhuff, R. R. *Empowering.* Amherst, MA: HRD Press, 1989.

Carkhuff, R. R. and Berenson, B. G. *The Possibilities Organization.* Amherst, MA: HRD Press, 2000.

Carkhuff, R. R., Carkhuff, C. J., and Cohen, B. *IP⁵D – Integrated Process Development: The Possibilities Business in the Possibilities Economy.* Amherst, MA: HRD Press, 2002.

Carkhuff, R. R., Carkhuff, C. J. and Kelly, J. T. *The GICCA Curve: The Possibilities Marketplace.* Amherst, MA: HRD Press, 2002.

Tisdale, D., Carkhuff, C. J. and Rayson, P. *The Colaré Model: Describing, Predicting and Prescribing Project Success.* Amherst, MA: HRD Press, 2002.

6. The Possibilities Community

by Andrew H. Griffin, D.Ed.
George Banks, Ph.D.
Karen Banks, Ph.D.
John A. Linder, D.Sc.
George Logan-El, Ph.D.
John Pope, M.Ed.

The Possibilities Community
MEANING

Communities are the generators of the components of freedom: **New Capital Development.** Communities are the sum of relationships among and between: homes and neighborhoods, schools and higher education, governance and business.

This chapter offers a research-based model for community effectiveness. Ultimately, every part of the community contributes to developing or applying *New Capital* within and between communities by: marketplace positioning, organizational alignment, human processing, information modeling, and mechanical tooling.

Springfield, Massachusetts, is the dominant city in western Massachusetts, with a population of approximately 160,000. In 1988, the city received widespread media attention for what **Newsweek** *described as* "**The Springfield Miracle —** Economic growth at the expense of the once-entrenched large-scale manufacturing." *Today, the city's industrial plants have been shutting down, but service industries and small-scale "job shops" have taken their place. The biggest growth has been in financial services, accounting firms, and insurance companies. All of these factors have converged to reduce unemployment to below 3 percent.*

There are many sources of this miraculous "**upturn.**" *Perhaps most important is the entrepreneurial initiative that was activated in the face of lost business. Supported by technological innovation that freed them of geographical boundaries, many entrepreneurs were attracted to the quality of life of western Massachusetts. In addition, the intrapreneurs of the largest Springfield-based insurance companies, Massachusetts Mutual (MassMutual) and Monarch Capital, created new financial service offerings and expanded their businesses severalfold.*

Twenty years earlier, companies like MassMutual and Monarch Life were deeply troubled about the future of Springfield. Like so many other cities in the Northeast at that time, Springfield — then a town of 178,000 — was a dying town. Many industries had fled South, seeking cheaper labor and leaving other labor — skilled and unskilled — behind to fend for itself. But Springfield was also a proud town. It considered itself the "City of Homes."

In the late 1960s, Springfield, like many cities around the nation, became involved in civil upheaval. There were periodic riots in the community as disenfranchised minorities challenged the Establishment for opportunities. Discontent spread to school-age youth where there was great unrest. During this period of upheaval, families were falling apart and neighborhoods that had once been extended families were becoming not only careless places to live but dangerous ones as well.

People like Jim Martin and Ben Jones, respective CEOs of MassMutual and Monarch, were concerned about the future prosperity of their companies and the welfare of their personnel. The minority communities were quickly surrounding their corporate headquarters. Riots were spreading from nearby Winchester Square toward the face-to-face locations of the insurance companies on State Street. Personnel like J. Walter Reardon, Vice President for Public Relations at MassMutual, realized that action needed to be taken. But what? To leave would be to abdicate their felt responsibilities to the community. To stay would be to face the unknown without solutions.

At this point, a serendipitous convergence of initiatives took place. American International College, a small liberal arts college, also found itself in the middle of the black and brown communities, half-way between Winchester Square and the State Street insurance centers. In the summer of 1967, Dr. Richard Sprinthall brought together Andrew H. Griffin, a community leader, and Drs. Carkhuff and Berenson to pilot-test some community training programs. Soon, then-vice-president Harry Corniotes saw the potentially unique contributions of a college-based human resource initiative and supported the establishment of the Center for Human Resource Development.

Our first analysis indicated that crises in the homes, schools, and businesses were debilitating a once-progressive city. Springfield met all of the conditions for social disorder enumerated by the Kerner Commission (National Advisory Commission, 1968). No one in the community had the skills to counteract social and economic regression. The parents did not have the skills to parent. The teachers did not have the skills to teach. The workers did not have the skills to work. The managers did not have the skills to manage. The entire community was dysfunctional.

When we initiated our community development program more than 35 years ago, we asked Carkhuff and Berenson, "How should we begin?" *Their answer:* "We begin by asking everyone in the community what they would like to do with the rest of their lives." *This was the essence of* **The Possibilities Community.** *It is also the essence of* **The Possibilities Governance.**

The responses of the thousands of marginalized people whose input we solicited were incredibly insightful and forgiving. They factored out to this: "We want to be every place that impacts us."

Translated, this meant both public-sector services and private-sector employment; it meant "womb-to-tomb" *services that would facilitate the growth and development of the community members.*

Ultimately, it meant a "Shadow Community" *to service those who were victims of, in Senator Moynihan's words,* "benign neglect." *The* "Shadow Community" *began with pre-parenting and parenting training; it extended from early childhood educational programs through elementary and secondary support systems to introductory college and specialized training experiences; it further extended to all governance services — housing, welfare, recreation — and all private sector activities — employment, banking, policymaking; it culminated in the second-*

career and retirement programs of those who lived their lives as gainfully employed and enlightened citizens.

For us, it was the policymaking level that was most highly leveraged. Accordingly, we created a graduate training program in human resource development and recruited leaders from both the private and public sectors to participate. In the nightly classrooms, we processed the issues of our time. In doing so, we empowered the marginalized community members to contribute to the creation of **The Possibilities Community.** *This is that story.*

The New Platform for Community

Until now, humankind has proceeded inductively by conceptualizing and operationalizing phenomena far beyond the reach of its brainpower. That is precisely why it has evolved so slowly. Now, humankind can proceed deductively to dimensionalize phenomena by modeling them. If we can model phenomena, then they will live for us: we can understand the relationships within, between, and among phenomena.

With applications in processing, we will conquer the systems that source our dimensional models. If phenomena can live for us, then we can conquer the substance of nature's systems, for they are but windows in space and time on directional forces in God's universes.

With dedication to transfers in processing, we can begin to understand the conditions of our systems. If we can conquer the substance of the systems, then we can begin to discriminate the multidimensional, interdependent, asymmetrical, and changeable processing systems of God's phenomenal universes.

In this context, **The New Science of Possibilities**, especially in its deductive processing form, is an accelerator of evolution for any and all phenomena. We can generate totally new initiatives in an afternoon, initiatives that formerly may have required millennia to evolve.

The New Science of Possibilities culminates in the dedication of all of our processing systems to releasing or freeing phenomena to seek their own destinies. Possibilities science is empowered by intervening to enhance phenomenal potential to express itself fully. It all begins with relating.

When we relate to the community's phenomenal processing system, we discover a community development system (see Figure 6-1):

- The human development **(HD)** functions of the homes and neighborhoods are to transform untutored humans into human potential **(HP)**.

- The human resource development **(HRD)** functions of the schools and training are to transform human potential into human resources **(HR)**.

- The human capital development **(HCD)** functions of higher education and science are to transform human resources into human capital capable of generating information capital **(HC $\leftrightarrow$ IC)**.

- The organizational capital development **(OCD)** functions of government and services are to emphasize investing human capital to generate organization capital **(OC)**.

- The marketplace capital development **(MCD)** functions of business are to emphasize transforming organization capital into marketplace capital **(MC)**.

Of course, all of these capital development operations are developmental and cumulative, as we will see shortly.

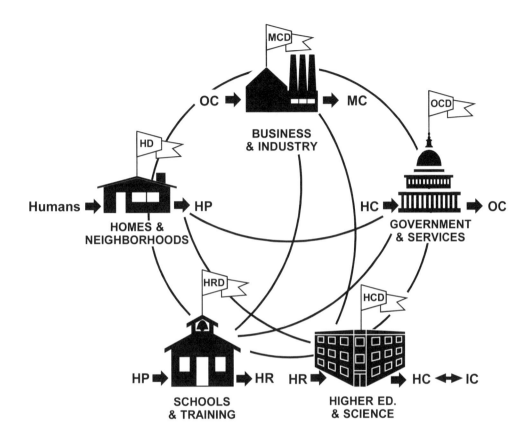

Figure 6-1. Community Development System

In Figure 6-2, we may view the new capital ingredients of community capital development. As may be noted, organizational capital is developed simultaneously with the new capital development processing systems:

- The **HD** delivery functions of the home are discharged by the production components enabled by **S–R** conditioned responding processes.

- The **HRD** supervisory function of the school are discharged by technological components enabled by **S–O–R** discriminative learning systems.

- The **HCD** ↔ **ICD** management functions of higher education are discharged by tailored resource integration components enabled by **S–P–R** generative processing systems.

- The **OCD** executive functions of governance are discharged by executive leadership components enabled by **S–OP–R** generative organizational processing systems.

- The **MCD** policymaking functions of business are discharged by marketing leadership components enabled by **S–MP–R** generative marketplace processing systems.

Again, all of these capital development operations are developmental and cumulative.

What is impressive is that there is a community development system. It appears magical. What is most impressive, however, is that there are models for new capital development that build the community systematically and cumulatively.

In turn, when the community is dedicated to the mission of governance capital development, it relates to other communities and cultures. At the highest levels, then, communities and governance relate interdependently with other communities and governance. This is mutual processing for mutual benefit, and it defines new capital development.

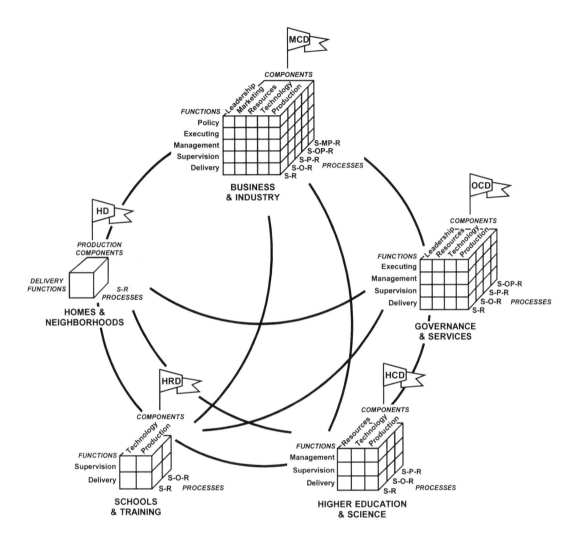

**Figure 6-2. Community Capital Development System —
New Capital Development**

This new capital development vision of community functions was not always so clear:

Berenson: Even though we began with the focus upon community capital development, we discovered the potential of cultural capital development.

Griffin: Cultural capital is found in how a community or a nation relates within itself and, also, how it relates to other cultures.

Berenson: Global possibilities cultures are defined in achievable terms …

Carkhuff: By cultural relating!

Griffin: Cultures that relate collaboratively or interdependently are healthy cultures.

Berenson: Just like people who relate interdependently!

Carkhuff: It remains for thinking people to define their own relationships as well as their cultures!

Griffin: It remains for thinking people to generate their own possibilities …

Berenson: … As well as those of future generations!

Griffin: That's what *The Possibilities Community* is all about— relating to generate possibilities.

CCD — Community Capital Development

In this context, *The Possibilities Community* generates community capital development, or **CCD.** As can be viewed in Figure 6-3, all dimensions of **CCD** are aligned to accomplish the **NCD** functions of community capital development. In this model, marketplace components as well as organizational processes emphasize **New Capital Development** or **NCD:**

- **MCD:** Marketplace Capital Development, or positioning in the marketplace;

- **OCD:** Organizational Capital Development, or organizational alignment with marketplace positioning;

- **HCD:** Human Capital Development, or human processing to implement organizational alignment;

- **ICD:** Information Capital Development, or information modeling to culminate human processing;

- **mCD:** Mechanical Capital Development, or mechanical tooling to implement information modeling.

Together, these sources define **NCD.**

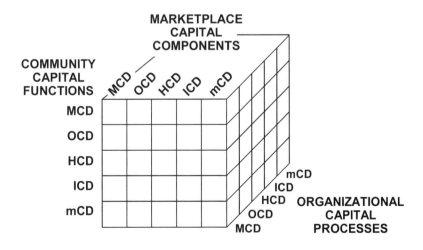

Figure 6-3. The Community Capital Development Model

Clearly, **CCD** generates **NCD:**

- **CCD** functions emphasize the **NCD** benefits that empower the capital development systems within which **CCD** is nested.

- **CCD** components emphasize the **MCD** systems that enable positioning in the marketplace based upon maximizing **NCD** requirements and capacities.

- **CCD** processes emphasize the **OCD** systems that generate **NCD** to align organizational resources with marketplace positioning.

In short, **CCD** is the generating engine that empowers governance, economics, and cultural capital development.

The HCD Mission

One of the missions of the **CCD** change program of 35 years ago was human capital development, or **HCD.** The principles of community capital development will be seen most vividly by taking an in-depth view of the **HCD** experience. Let us begin with a definition of **HCD** that still eludes our private- and public-sector policymakers.

At the most basic level, **HCD** is defined by the development of physical, emotional, and intellectual resources. Even the ancient Greeks understood this. However, the true definition of **HCD** comes not so much in the ingredients as in the mathematical arrangement of the ingredients:

$$\textbf{HCD} \ = \ \textbf{P} \bullet \textbf{E}^2 \bullet \textbf{I}^5$$

HCD is defined by the interaction and the power of its dimensions: physical development is multiplied by the square of our emotional development; in turn, these factors are multiplied by our intellectual development to the 5th power. More powerful than the formula is the meaning we ascribe to it.

Exponential algebra tells it all. The real power of **HCD** is in the intellect. "$\textbf{I}^5$" reduces the other dimensions to support functions. In other words, it is our intellect that makes us *"capital":* our ability to think or generate new and productive ideas. Our physical fitness serves to *energize* our efforts. Our emotional fitness serves to *catalyze* our efforts. But it is our intellectual fitness that serves to *actualize* our efforts! In a word, **HCD** is *brainpower.*

In perspective, **HCD** is a lifelong process. It begins with the maturity of parents and the care and nourishment of their children in utero. It emphasizes friendly biochemistry fostered by the love and stimulation directed to children in infancy. It continues in adolescence with facilitative learning culminating in instrumentally learned objectives. It is powered in adulthood by systematic thinking skills programs that are applied and transferred in all contexts. It culminates in maturity in the generation of *breakthrough* ideas, innovation in new forms of applications, and commercialization in new products and services. To sum, **HCD** is a lifelong learning process that contributes the driving ideas in any equation for generating wealth.

Beginning nearly 35 years ago, then, we who worked on the Springfield project set up **HCD** programs to empower unemployed and disenfranchised minorities to become mainstreamed and gainfully employed citizens. We had a more limited vision of human capital potential than we do now. We clearly saw the multiplicative effects of physical, emotional, and intellectual resources. However, in emphasizing the emotional dimensions of motivating and relating, we underestimated the extraordinary power of the intellect. Nevertheless, we called our **HCD** participants *"90-day wonders!"* Their transformation from raw resources into invaluable human resources was profound.

First, we went to the people themselves and asked them where they wanted to be. They answered intelligently: *"Every place that impacts us!"*

Next, we approached the private and public sectors in order to provide opportunities in literally all the desired areas. We defined all of the tasks to be performed, and designed training programs to empower the people in task performance.

Finally, we utilized the resources of the people themselves. The highest-functioning trainees of each wave were selected to train the next wave before being placed on jobs themselves. Human relations specialists eased the transitions of workers-to-jobs and students-to-school. People who were promoted or sought new employment replaced themselves before leaving their jobs.

In short, the **HCD** participants were *surrounded.* **HCD** programs permeated every area of the Springfield community. We became a family. The **HCD** family!

However, while the participants were surrounded by areas of **HCD** applications, the effective ingredient in community culture change was the **HCD** program itself. We *penetrated* to the very souls of individual participants by developing and implementing tailored **HCD** programs:

- Physical fitness programs that enhanced their health and energy;

- Emotional fitness programs that elevated their motivation and interpersonal relating skills;

- Intellectual fitness programs that empowered them with skills in goal defining, content learning, decision making, and program development.

The actuarial results were incredible. One hundred percent job placement! Over 80% gainfully employed 25 years later (this against projected success rates in the 15% range)! Fifty percent of **HCD** graduates went on to receive college degrees (this from a group that began the program averaging less than an eighth grade education)! No incidents of criminality! No welfare recipients! Productive citizens all! Perhaps most important, no violent deaths in Springfield! Of all the northern cities troubled by violence in the 1960s, only Springfield remained unscathed.

Still more powerful than the quantitative data were the qualitative data. From the ranks of the unemployed and disenfranchised came numerous participants, contributors, and leaders in both the private and public sectors, including the following:

- A member of the board of directors of a Fortune 500 firm (this a formerly unemployed person);

- A state director of institutional services in youth corrections (this a former delinquent);

- An associate dean of admissions at a prominent Ivy League-type women's college (this a former welfare mother);

- A state senator, presiding over the House Ways and Means Committee (now retired);

- Graduates of MIT, Harvard, and other prominent universities (including a welfare mother);

- Two multi-millionaires!

Need we say more?!

There is more! What was so impressive was how far the **HCD** graduates went. We began with known targets of entry-level jobs working on production lines and making service deliveries. The graduates expanded their aspirations and went on to totally new and elevated fields of endeavor. They looked beyond the *high beams!*

As one preeminent psychologist remarked upon studying the before-and-after **HCD** profiles: *"These are not the same people — they are qualitatively different people now than they were upon entry to* **HCD.***"*

We did all of this by empowering the participants with **HCD** skills. By replacing destructive criminal career ladders with constructive community career ladders! By replacing criminal justice with community justice!

There is a footnote to this story of community development. As mentioned earlier, in the 1980s the city was promoted nationally in the media as *"The Springfield Miracle."* Today, however, like most of the communities in America, Springfield faces a similar transition. It has lost its sources of growth in the global information economy. It must search out the new sources of economic growth and reposition itself in the changing requirements. Once again, it must develop new and more powerful community capital.

The Possibilities Vision

So what of the future? What is our vision for community capital development? Put another way, what would we be doing now — 35 years later — if called upon to reengineer Springfield again? Thanks to the continued work of

Carkhuff and Berenson, we would begin with the most powerful sources of capital development:

- More powerful designs for integrating community components to relate to marketplace positioning **(CCD)**;

- More powerful designs for positioning in the marketplace **(MCD)**;

- More powerful designs for reengineering organizations and their customers **(OCD)**;

- More powerful designs for empowering humans **(HCD)**;

- More powerful designs for generating productive information **(ICD)**;

- More powerful designs for generating productive mechanical tools **(mCD)**.

Ultimately, all of these capital sources relate interdependently in an equation for generating spiraling growth in wealth. This equation may be conceived of as community capital development: *a wealth-generating community that develops and relates all capital sources of wealth.*

CCD — Community Capital Development

First, we have more powerful designs for community capital development, or **CCD.** In Springfield, we surrounded and penetrated all programs in all components of the community — from early childhood education through public education, welfare, housing, recreation, justice, corrections, and higher education to corporations and governmental agencies. We did this by relating to each component and relating the components systematically to each other.

Viewing each component in the community as a capital development system in its own right, we related all components interdependently. For example, we encouraged private corporations to put contracting work out on bids to public-sector profit centers. This did not interfere with their free market enterprise; rather, it facilitated it by opening up contracting to Third World subcultures existing within the American community. In return, both the private and public sectors became recipients of extraordinary levels of other capital such as human and information capital.

Again, the central paradigm in **CCD** is the same relationship between the marketplace and the community. Too often, the various components of the community tend to believe that they exist independently for their own purposes. Often, they do not understand their symbiotic relationship to the marketplace until it is too late. Communities grow and die with this relationship. They grow when they align to accomplish a marketplace mission. They die when they do not.

MCD — Marketplace Capital Development

Second, we have more powerful designs for marketplace capital development, or **MCD.** In Springfield, we empowered majority leaders to prepare for the changing economic requirements and the minority community to relate to the emerging markets as perceived by the majority leaders. Except informally, such as in person-to-person communications, we made little effort to relate communities to each other in order to develop marketplace capital.

Clearly, an interdependent marketplace paradigm applies to relations between communities: we would now relate communities interdependently in the larger marketplace. Alternating as producers and consumers, these communities contribute to each other's growth. In other words, it is insufficient to develop community capital without reference to the economy. Indeed, the vitality of both are intimately bound together: the community and the marketplace. It is a very limited view of marketing to sell exclusively to individuals and organizations. The dominant markets of the 21st century global economy will be in the communities themselves. Indeed, leveraged marketing is to be found in relating interdependently to entire communities. To be sure, the most leveraged marketing is between the communities. This is not simply a version of *"Win-Win"* — negotiated benefits between independent and competitive entities. This is a vision of *"Grow-Grow"* — an interdependent relationship between collaborators.

The central paradigm in **MCD** is the relationship between marketplace and community culture. Throughout American history, community culture has co-existed with market culture as integral parts of society. Indeed, in the 1970s and early 1980s, guided by leaders of the great American corporations like IBM and AT&T, the corporate world attempted to integrate the two cultures of marketplace and community. Certainly, for a moment in time, our corporate leaders saw these two cultures as one and the same. Then they were *blind-sided* in the 1980s by the command economy of Japan operating in a free market: manipulating internal alliances, and playing for market share rather than profit in a free-market context. The American corporations mobilized to become fiercely competitive. They restructured their organizations and downsized their human resources. They chose the market culture — exclusively! The implications for community culture continue to be profound. Thankfully, the leaders can choose again.

OCD — Organizational Capital Development

Third, we have more powerful designs for organizational capital development, or **OCD.** In Springfield, we related to organizations in the private and public sectors the same way we related to individuals. We attempted to be helpful to their leaders in making the organizations more effective. But we made no attempt to change the organizations systematically.

We would now work with the people to realign their organizations systematically. We would design cost-beneficial systems within every area of endeavor. This would include the public sector as well as the private sector. For example, we would reposition our education, welfare, justice, and other systems as profit centers — to be run as profitable businesses. In other words, each center would be built around ongoing as well as new *start-up* businesses. Within each center, every **HCD** participant would have the opportunity to perform (for pay) at progressively skilled levels of functioning, from delivery to policymaking. Moreover, each matured participant would have the opportunity and support to generate plans for entrepreneurial *start-ups* or intrapreneurial expansions. All learning in these centers would be instrumental to successful functioning in the 21st century economy.

The central paradigm in **OCD** is organizational alignment. We envision continuous organizational alignment throughout the 21st century and, indeed, the remainder of human history, if we are to have a good one. Organizational alignment begins with continuously reorienting the organization to meet its constantly changing customer requirements. In turn, the organization is continuously "rearchitected" to meet the changing requirements. This architectural process is extended and recycled as the customers of customers are continuously rearchitected.

HCD — Human Capital Development

Fourth, we have more powerful **HCD** goals than we had 35 years ago. In our **HCD** programs, we prepared our participants to perform specific, existing jobs. In other words, we lobbied the private and public sectors to match their needs with our resources. We accepted the economic realities as they existed and trained our people to respond to them.

Today, we are confronted with spiraling economic changes. Corporations are constantly restructured; entire industries come into and go out of existence in a matter of years. The average person will change not just jobs but entire careers several times in their lives. For this 21st century marketplace, we empower our **HCD** participants for entrepreneurial initiative. Whereas our earlier programs emphasized responding to economic realities, our current program emphasizes initiating new economic realities: entrepreneurial initiative in evolving and expanding existing organizations; entrepreneurial initiative in creating new organizations!

The central paradigm in **HCD** goaling, then, is initiative. We are entering a grand Age of Entrepreneurism. By the year 2005, more than one-half of our workforce will be contractors and subcontractors operating out of their homes and small field offices. There will be no letup as we evolve to an entrepreneurial-driven, free enterprise economy. In response to the increasing complexities of the information economy, the new initiatives will take the form of joint ventures, partnerships, and strategic alliances as entrepreneurism is redefined as interdependent rather than independent initiatives.

ICD — Information Capital Development

Fifth, we have more powerful technologies than we had in our programs of 35 years ago. Responding to the communication requirements of the emerging Data Age, we emphasized the interpersonal tools of relating people, data, and things. For example, we would teach people to attend and respond to their worlds and the people in them. This helped people relate more effectively to their families, their learning tasks, their job performance.

Drawn from the increasingly intellectual requirements of the Information Age, our **ICD** tools are exponentially more powerful than they were earlier. For example, we can now teach people to represent information operationally—any information! Moreover, we can empower them to transform it systematically into more productive information. This will enable people to process the changing requirements of their constantly changing environments.

The central paradigm in **ICD** is *empowering*. Empowering is not defined simply by ceding political or managerial power. In fact, empowering is defined in the synergistic or mutual growth-producing relationship between **ICD** and other capital development systems: as **ICD** is elevated, the other systems are empowered. For example, empowering is found in enabling individuals to process any contextual environment productively. Instead of consultants coming in to conquer our systems and design new ones, we are enabled to design our own systems. In other words, we learn to manage our own destinies.

mCD—Mechanical Capital Development

Finally, we have more powerful mechanical technologies than we had in our programs of 35 years ago. Back then, our machines and tools were dysfunctional, designed for another time and another economy. All that we could do was prepare the other sources of growth; then, they could converge upon designing their own new mechanical tools.

Today, we are blessed with a multitude of mechanical hardware systems, including integrated computer systems that process quantitative data far more rapidly (and qualitative information far less often) than humans require; telecommunication systems that do everything but transport us bodily to our partners; and *CAD-CAM* processes that enable us to accelerate the manufacturing processes through *virtual product development*. Indeed, we have the mechanical technologies to do virtually anything we choose. Let us rephrase that: we have the information-technology-driven mechanical technologies to do anything we choose—virtually! The problem is what we choose.

The central paradigm in **mCD** is the generating system. It is not the mechanical system that produces our products; it is the contextual systems that produce our mechanical systems. To be most useful and powerful, our mechanical technologies must be driven deductively by more powerful capital development systems; the **ICD** that drives our **MCD** requirements; the **HCD** that drives our **ICD** requirements; the **OCD** that drives our **HCD** requirements; the **CCD** that drives our **OCD** requirements; the **MCD** that drives our **CCD** requirements. Then and only then will we have hardware that is truly **mCD.**

These, then, are the powerful principles of community capital development:

- **CCD** as the interdependently related components of the community that produce **NCD;**

- **MCD** as the interdependent positioning of communities in the marketplace;

- **OCD** as continuous and interdependent reengineering within and between organizations and their customer organizations;

- **HCD** as interdependent intrapreneurial and entrepreneurial initiators;

- **ICD** as interdependent information-building tools for empowering other sources of capital development;

- **mCD** as state-of-the-art machinery and tools dedicated interdependently to implementing the capital development systems.

The community is the generating engine for the production of the **NCD** that empowers governance.

Clearly, the operative word in all of these principles is *"interdependent."* Interdependency is defined as *mutual processing for mutual benefit.* In point of fact, interdependency defines all of these new and emerging capital development systems. Indeed, it is only when all of these systems are related interdependently that we develop governance capital development.

Viewed in information terms, then, we are already a global village. All entities are incorporated within our borders. No entities are beyond our reach. Moreover, all entities are related in ways that are, increasingly, determined by marketplace information. We may conceive of this marketplace information as the evolving requirements for survival and growth in the global marketplace.

The most powerful principle of the Springfield experience of *The Possibilities Community* was the *"bridging"* principle of disaster averted and collaboration enacted. In the late 1960s, racial warfare was ubiquitous throughout the northern cities of America. Springfield was on the verge of violence when white youth drove through "the Hill" firing weapons at blacks and browns.

Having great difficulty in "keeping the lid" on the violent reaction to this intrusion, Andrew H. Griffin, local leader of the **National Association for the Advancement of Colored People** committed an act of grace. He invited the leader of the **White Citizen's Group** to meet him at NAACP headquarters to process with him on the welfare of their children—the mutual *"bridge"* to which they were both committed.

This was perhaps the first act of collaborative relating that had taken place in Springfield, at least, and perhaps the first in any community. The two leaders met. They processed interdependently — *"mutual processing for mutual benefit."* They made a commitment to community peace and economic growth. They pledged themselves to each other in the name of their extended community families. The rest, they say, is history.

Of all the northern cities in the country, Springfield never had a violent fatality during this period. Threats of violence were treated in ways that emphasized relating. For example, when rioting between white and minority youth threatened Technical High School, Griffin sent in two human-relations specialists to replace more than 50 police officers on the scene. The youth parted like the seas before Moses. The specialists, Maurita Bledsoe and Ronnie Carroll, were well recognized for their relating skills. They divided the races down into racially homogeneous groups for training in relating skills before bringing them together in mixed groups for skills applications.

There never was another racial incident. ***The Possibilities Community*** lives on in the matured hearts, minds, and souls of those who were in Springfield during those troubled times. Seemingly lost in fires of unrelatedness, Springfield rose like the ancient phoenix from the ashes to become something more than it was intended to be — something possibilistic! It established the model for relating in the 21st century community. The miracle of relating!

In summary, the Springfield *"miracle"* was a transformation from a dying and dysfunctional industrial community to a growthful and productive information community. There were many sources of this "miracle." Perhaps most important was the minority community's readiness to perform and relate to the majority community. The source of this readiness was thinking people — ready to think, relate, and plan. The source of thinking people was a human technology. The product of this readiness was a thinking community — ready to relate interdependently with all of its constituents.

Perhaps ***The Possibilities Community*** was best summarized by Walter Reardon in his graduate thesis:

> *We must dispose of the notion that change is a process that alters the tranquil status quo — because in the area of community change, there is no tranquility at all.* (Carkhuff and Reardon, 1971)

References

Carkhuff, R. R. *The Development of Human Resources.* New York: Holt, Rinehart & Winston, 1971.

Carkhuff, R. R., Aspy, D.N., Benoit, D., and Griffin, A. H. *The Possibilities Schools Series.* Amherst, MA: HRD Press, 2002.

Carkhuff, R. R., Griffin, A. H., and Berenson, B. G. *The Possibilities Community.* Amherst, MA: HRD Press, 2002.

Carkhuff, R. R. and Reardon, J. W. "Industry and the Development of Human Resources." Chapter in L. E. Abt and B. F. Reiss (Eds.), *Progress in Clinical Psychology.* New York: Grune & Stratton, 1971.

Moynihan, D. P. "Making Welfare Work." Washington, DC: Senate Committee on National Advisory Commission, *Report on Civil Disorders.* New York: Bantam Books, 1968.

National Advisory Commission. *Report on Civil Disorders.* New York: Bantam Books, 1968.

Nocera, J. "The Springfield Miracle." *Newsweek,* June 6, 1988, pp. 45–48.

III. The Freedom-Building Systems

7. The Freedom Functions

by Robert R. Carkhuff, Ph.D.
Bernard G. Berenson, Ph.D.
Rob Owen, M.B.A.

The Freedom Functions
MEANING

Civilization can be measured by a society's *Freedom-Building Systems*. An analysis of these systems begins with an analysis of *The Freedom Functions*:

- **Interdependent Cultural Relating**
- **Free Enterprise Economics**
- **Direct Democratic Governance**

When we view nations through the lens of *The Freedom Functions* we find that those nations that are committed to these three functions are the most productive and the most free. Conversely, we find that those nations that are least committed to these three functions are the least productive and the least free.

This chapter provides perspective and a summary of research regarding the interrelated role of governance and enterprise: the less the government imposes burdens upon economics, the more free and profitable the enterprise.

The Freedom Functions

Economic freedom is essential to the three main **Freedom Functions** presented in our introduction to this chapter. By assessing economic freedom, we may expand upon, or further detail, our functions. In this area, there is perhaps no greater source of information than The Heritage Foundation, a research and educational institute whose efforts to assess economic freedom have perhaps no peer. It's *Index of Economic Freedom,* produced since 1995, is a leading guide to the world's economies, offering "the broadest array of institutional factors determining economic freedom" (O'Driscoll, Feulner, and O'Grady, 2003).

Defining freedom as *"the absence of government coercion or constraint upon the production, distribution, or consumption of goods and services beyond the extent necessary for citizens to protect and maintain liberty itself,"* the Heritage researchers assessed each of ten broad factors from 1 to 5 on individualized scales. Scores for the factors could then be added and averaged, with an overall composite score assigned to each country as follows:

- **Free or Unconstrained** — countries with average overall scores of 1.95 or less;

- **Mostly Free** — countries with an average overall score of 2.00 to 2.95;

- **Mostly Unfree** — countries with an average overall score of 3.00 to 3.95;

- **Unfree or Repressed** — countries with an average overall score of 4.0 or higher.

To sum, the researchers examined some 50 independent variables — five for each of the ten factors — to determine the overall level of economic freedom.

In so doing, the researchers established a powerful relationship between economic-freedom factors and economic prosperity. There are significant differences between the **Free Nations** and the **Unfree Nations** on performance indices such as per capita **Gross Domestic Product** or **GDP.** Succinctly stated, **Free Nations** prosper with **GDPs** that are multiples of those of **Unfree Nations.**

Each country can thus be graded on the ten factors of economic freedom:

1. **Trade Policy** measures the degree to which government hinders the free flow of foreign commerce in such a manner as to discourage free enterprise initiative. For example, with non-tariff barriers such as import bans and quotas, the weighted average tariffs range from four percent or less for low scores (Level 1) to more than 19 percent for high scores (Level 5).

2. **Fiscal Burdens** of government include income and corporate tax rates as well as government expenditures that discourage free enterprise initiative. For example, the average of income tax rates ranges from zero percent (Level 1) to more than 50 percent (Level 5).

3. **Government Intervention** measures the government's direct use of scarce resources in such a manner so as to constrict economic freedom. For example, the average of government expenditures ranges from less than 15 percent (Level 1) to more than 30 percent (Level 5).

4. **Monetary Policy** measures the value of a country's currency, which either facilitates or retards individual economic freedom. For example, the average of inflation rates ranges from less than three percent (Level 1) to more than 20 percent (Level 5).

5. **Capital Flows** measure the limits on inflow of foreign investment that hamper economic freedom. For example, the average of barriers to foreign investment ranges from open and impartial treatment (Level 1) to active prevention (Level 5).

6. **Banking and Finance** measure government control of banks and, thus, financial transactions that hinder allocation to their highest use. For example, the average of restrictions on banks ranges from negligible government involvement (Level 1) to state-owned banking enterprises (Level 5).

7. **Wages and Prices** measure government intervention in wages and prices that hinder the allocation of financial resources to their highest use. For example, the average of wage and price controls ranges from market-driven (Level 1) to government controlled (Level 5).

8. **Property Rights** measure the rule of law and the ability to accumulate private property, which is the primary motivating force in the free enterprise economy. For example, the average of property rights ranges from government protection (Level 1) to government accumulation (Level 5).

9. **Regulation** measures the freedom or restriction in licensing new businesses that have facilitative or retarding effects upon free enterprise initiatives. For example, the average of regulations ranges from straightforward and expeditious (Level 1) to direct impediments to the creation of new business (Level 5).

10. **Black Market** measures the effect of government intervention in the marketplace through taxing or some other regulatory burdens, thus capturing the indirect effects of government intervention upon free enterprise. For example, the average of black market activities ranges from very low levels in free economies (Level 1) to very high levels in unfree economies (Level 5).

In perspective, the ten factors and 50 indices emphasize governmental activities that facilitate or retard free economic enterprise. They are not, themselves, indices of the governance processes for generating initiatives that enhance or constrain free enterprise. To obtain these indices, we must study the nature of governance processes, ranging from totalitarian to free democratic. Nor are these ten factors indices of economic performance. To obtain performance indices, we must study the relationships of these broad factors with individual, or per capita, **GDP.**

The Freedom Outcomes

The 156 nations analyzed are grouped according to their composite averages for each of the ten economic functions: trade policy, fiscal burden, government intervention, monetary policy, foreign investment (capital flows), banking and finance, wages and prices, property rights, regulation, and black market. For example, in Table 7-1, the 15 nations with composite scores of 1.95 or lower are rated as **"Free"** in *The Index of Economic Freedom* rankings.

Table 7-1. Freedom Scores and Economies of Free Nations

Nation	Freedom Scores	GDP (PPP)	GDP (1995 $)
Hong Kong	1.45	$ 25,153	$ 24,218
Singapore	1.50	$ 23,356	$ 28,230
Luxemburg	1.70	$ 50,061	$ 56,372
New Zealand	1.70	$ 20,070	$ 17,548
Ireland	1.75	$ 29,866	$ 27,741
Denmark	1.80	$ 27,627	$ 38,521
Estonia	1.80	$ 10,066	$ 4,431
U.S.A.	1.80	$ 34,142	$ 31,996
Australia	1.85	$ 25,693	$ 23,838
United Kingdom	1.85	$ 23,509	$ 21,667
Finland	1.90	$ 24,996	$ 32,024
Iceland	1.90	$ 29,581	$ 31,304
Netherlands	1.90	$ 25,657	$ 30,967
Sweden	1.90	$ 24,277	$ 31,206
Switzerland	1.95	$ 28,769	$ 46,737

As may be noted, Hong King and Singapore received the best **"Free"** scores: 1.45 and 1.5 respectively. The other **"Free"** scores range from 1.7 to 1.95. With the exception of Estonia, a former Soviet Satellite country that has dedicated itself to economic freedom, the countries have a legacy of economic freedom. At the same time, with the exception of Hong Kong and Singapore, even **"Free"** nations continue to be inhibited in their freedom by burdens of government intervention.

In turn, the 11 nations with composite scores over 4.00 are rated as **"Unfree"** (Table 7-2). All of these nations carry extraordinary burdens for all economic functions.

Table 7-2. Freedom Scores and Economies of Unfree Nations

Nation	Freedom Scores	GDP (PPP)	GDP (1995 $)
Iran	4.15	$ 5,884	$ 1,649
Turkmenistan	4.15	$ 3,956	$ 1,377
Burma	4.20	$ 1,500	$ 144
Uzbekistan	4.25	$ 2,441	$ 767
Yugoslavia	4.25	$ 2,300	$ 1,240
Belarus	4.30	$ 7,544	$ 2,760
Libya	4.30	$ 8,900	$ ---
Laos	4.40	$ 1,575	$ 450
Zimbabwe	4.40	$ 2,635	$ 621
Cuba	4.45	$ 1,700	$ ---
North Korea	5.00	$ 1,000	$ ---

As may also be noted in Tables 7-1 and 7-2, the **Per Capital GDP** is calculated based upon two indices of purchasing power:

- **Purchasing Power Parity,** or **"PPP,"** is **GDP** converted to international dollars that have the same purchasing power as the U.S. dollar has in the United States.

- **Constant 1995 U.S. Dollars,** or **"1995 $,"** refers to **GDP** in U.S. dollars for the year 2000 adjusted for inflation using the 1995 **GDP** deflator.

In this context, the **Free Nations' Per Capital GDP** ranges roughly as follows for the two indices:

- **PPP** — between $10,000 and $50,000;

- **1995 $** — between $4,000 and $56,000.

In turn, the **Unfree Nations' Per Capita GDP** ranges loosely as follows:

- **PPP**—between $1,000 and $9,000;

- **1995 $**—between $144 and $2,760.

The contrast in economic performance between **Free** and **Unfree Nations** is made vivid by these data.

Freedom Implications

There is no overlap between the curves of the Free and Unfree economies! In other words, there are no instances in which the **GDPs** of one may fall into the curve of the **GDPs** of the other. This means that the differences between the populations are statistically significant. Highly significant! Such an **"overlap phenomenon"** is likely to occur randomly in less than one in a thousand instances!

The implications are profound! If a nation desires to become politically free and economically prosperous, it must address economic freedom. It must view the indices of the factors as objectives to be achieved in order to elevate prosperity.

Moreover, the aspiring nations must address the vehicles by which they can accomplish **The Freedom Functions.** We have summarized these dimensions as the **New Capital Development (NCD) Components:**

- **Marketplace Capital,** or marketplace positioning;
- **Organizational Capital,** or organizational alignment;
- **Human Capital,** or human processing;
- **Information Capital,** or information modeling;
- **Mechanical Capital,** or mechanical tooling.

Our analysis indicates that these **NCD Components** empower nations to accomplish **The Freedom Functions.** We will comment further in the next chapter.

The statistical significance of the difference pales in comparison with the functional significance! The mean **GDP** of the **Free Nations** is nearly 30 times that of the **Unfree Nations.** The **Free Nations'** peoples are freed politically to initiate entrepreneurially to generate still greater prosperity. The **Unfree Nations'** peoples are chained by tradition or totalitarianism that seeks only to control the distribution of what they cannot generate: **wealth!**

What about the more than 100 nations in the middle? Some are scrambling to become prosperous — like the former Soviet Satellites of Latvia and Lithuania. They have in mind objectives outlined by **The Freedom Functions.** They may find their destinies in the model of Estonia!

Others, like Venezuela and Brazil, are dependent and reactive. They attempt to become prosperous by rejecting or nullifying **The Freedom Functions.** They may find their destinies in the model of Cuba!

Yergin and Stanislaw have a message for the undecided in their book, *The Commanding Heights:*

- The truncation of Communism!
- The attenuation of Socialism!
- The commoditization of Parasitic Capitalism that is disposed only to subsidization and regulation!

Only the **Entrepreneurially-Driven, Free Enterprise Systems** that are disposed to the generation, innovation, and commercialization of breakthroughs in the marketplace will survive and grow in the 21st century free-enterprise marketplace!

In summary, only free and processing humans will generate the breakthrough ideas needed to initiate new markets. They will find powerful and trustworthy allies who will sponsor **The Freedom Functions!** And they will view their destinies in the models of the society of **Free Nations:** freely relating, freely enterprising, freely governing.

References

Carkhuff, R. R. and Berenson, B. G. *The New Science of Possibilities. Volumes I and II.* Amherst, MA: HRD Press, 2000.

Carkhuff, R. R. and Berenson, B.G. *The Possibilities Organization.* Amherst, MA: HRD Press, 2000.

Carkhuff, R. R. and Berenson, B.G. *The Possibilities Economics.* Amherst, MA: HRD Press, 2002.

International Monetary Fund. *Government Finance Statistics Yearbook. Vol. XXV.* Washington, DC: I.M.F., 2001.

O'Driscoll, G. P., Feulner, E. J., and O'Grady, M. A. *2003 Index of Economic Freedom.* Washington, DC: Heritage Foundation, 2003.

O'Driscoll, G. P., Holmes, K. R., and O'Grady, M. A. *2002 Index of Economic Freedom.* Washington, DC: Heritage Foundation, 2002.

Yergin, D. and Stanislaw, J. *The Commanding Heights: The Battle for the World Economy.* New York: Simon and Schuster, 2002.

8. The New Capital Components
by Robert R. Carkhuff, Ph.D.
Bernard G. Berenson, Ph.D.
Donald M. Benoit, M.Ed.

The New Capital Components
MEANING

The Freedom Functions are accomplished by *The New Capital Development (NCD) Components*:

- **MCD** or **Marketplace Capital Development**
- **OCD** or **Organization Capital Development**
- **HCD** or **Human Capital Development**
- **ICD** or **Information Capital Development**
- **mCD** or **Mechanical Capital Development**

Synergistically related, *The NCD Components* are the enabling source of all higher-order socioeconomic and sociopolitical development.

This chapter presents both the historical and futuristic roles of each of these *New Capital* ingredients which enable economic freedom. This chapter provides a succinct vision of the future of economic productivity: one where finances reduce to their value as catalysts and ways of "keeping score" while economic productivity is driven by *New Capital Development*.

The New Capital Components

If we follow the evolution of the modern organization, we can discover the sources of **New Capital Development.**

- First, companies added the *Chief Technology Officer;* then they added the *Chief Information Officer.*

- Now they are elevating the *Directors of Human Resource Development* and *Organizational Development.*

- Soon, if not yet, we will be including the *Director of Strategic Positioning* and perhaps even a *Director of Industry Positioning* or a *Director of Community Positioning.*

These elevations or appointments follow the evolution of the modern marketplace. They emphasize the sources of **New Capital Development** or **NCD:**

- **mCD — Mechanical Capital Development,**

- **ICD — Information Capital Development,**

- **HCD — Human Capital Development,**

- **OCD — Organization Capital Development,**

- **MCD — Marketplace Capital Development.**

They are the sources of our growth. They are dedicated to **The Freedom Functions** of **The Freedom Doctrine.**

Possibilities Economics builds upon historical sources of wealth generation and projects evolving and future sources. We begin constructing our model of such economics by tracing the evolutionary march of *"technological breakthroughs"* that have driven our economy. From the broadest perspective, economic growth in the marketplace and comparative advantage for organizations are driven by *"breakthroughs in technology development."* Agrarian technologies of seeding and herding were early *breakthroughs,* with agrarian methods and tools operating as sources of economic growth and comparative advantage. These technologies transformed the nomadic tribes of our hunter-gatherer ancestors into farming communities of agricultural people. In a similar manner, industrial machinery and systems transformed farming communities into industrial organizations. As we will see, new technologies are now changing our industrial organizations.

Relatedly, it is not until new *"breakthrough technologies"* are developed that the contributions of earlier technologies to wealth creation are fully realized, or *"capitalized."* For example, we did not actualize, or *"capitalize,"* the benefits of our agrarian technologies until we developed mechanical technologies to mechanize our agricultural practices. Similarly, we did not *"capitalize"* the productivity of our mechanical technologies until we developed information technologies to drive our machines. Likewise, we will not *"capitalize"* the potential of our information technologies until we develop human technologies to empower and free innovation. Moreover, we will not *"capitalize"* our human technologies until we develop organizational technologies to align our organizations. Finally, we will not *"capitalize"* the impact of organizational technologies until we have developed marketplace technologies to help us position our organizations in the marketplace.

Mechanical Capital Development

The mechanical-technology marketplace is the market of machinery and the products and services delivered by machines. The comparative benefits of mechanical technologies peaked at the height of the Industrial Age, and have all but disappeared due to the standardization of mechanical operations. From this perspective, we may view the decline of **Mechanical Technologies (mT)** as a source of comparative advantage, or *"competitive edge,"* for organizations (see Figure 8-1).

Manufacturing processes typically rely on some form of the mechanical assembly line. All companies automate their machinery to the maximum. All install statistical process controls to maximize the quality of machine outputs. In short, everyone who is dedicated to being equal is becoming equal in the mechanical production of off-the-shelf products for customers.

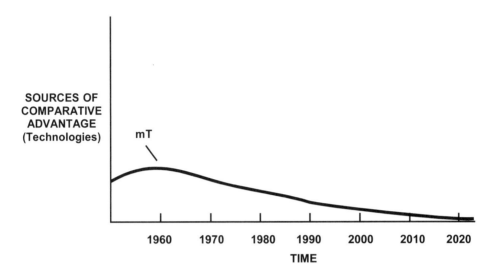

Figure 8-1. Market Impact of Mechanical Technologies (mT)

By choosing to offer our customers products and services through manu-facturing processes, we are choosing to position ourselves in an attenuating market. Without *breakthroughs,* mechanical technologies will continue to decline as a source of comparative advantage. Basically, this means a *level playing field* for everyone: if we are willing to make the investment in machinery and information systems to drive our machines, we can compete for declining profits. This is not to say that the market for mechanical and even agricultural products and services is not huge: it represents several trillion dollars globally, and there is still much money to be made. It is to say that many mechanical technologies have been around since the Industrial Age and simply yield the *least competitive edge.*

Whether or not we choose to define our organizations as mechanical operations, every organization is impacted by its ability to manage mechani-cal technologies. At the production or delivery levels, in particular, there is a great need to understand mechanical technologies and their applications.

The **mCD** process is one of the five sources of wealth generation that we have identified as critical for every organization to manage. The process allows us to start building our **New Capital Development (NCD) Equation**

for Wealth Generation, a formula that is valid for the 21st century and beyond. With *breakthroughs* in **mCD,** the equation for wealth becomes redefined (see Figure 8-2).

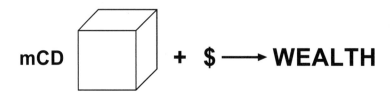

Figure 8-2. Wealth Driven by Mechanical Capital

Mechanical capital development is its own source of wealth. In an economy empowered by **mCD** technologies, it is mechanical capital that drives the production of products and services in the marketplace.

Information Capital Development

The information-technology marketplace is the market of information products and services. Themselves products of *breakthroughs* in electronics, **Information Technologies (IT)** climaxed as sources of comparative advantage in the 1980s. While driving our mechanical technologies to actualize their contributions, today's information technologies are also diminishing as a source of comparative advantage (see Figure 8-3). While their innovation potential remains infinite, their current comparative advantage is receding as the marketplace experiences the *"leveling"* effects of the near-instantaneous dissemination of information. Although the total size of the **IT** marketplace continues to grow, this dissemination has limited the competitive advantage of information technologies, since most companies now have access to reasonably priced, off-the-shelf and customized hardware and software, as well as a wide circulation of information.

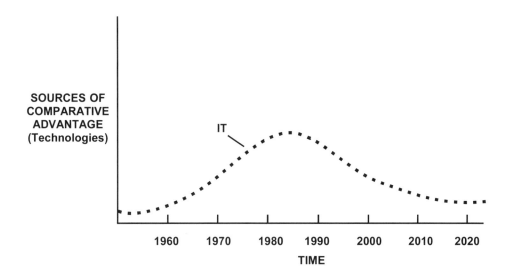

Figure 8-3. Market Impact of Information Technologies (IT)

By choosing to define our organizations as IT businesses, such as computer hardware, software, or publishing, we are choosing to position ourselves in a commoditizing market curve.

Current corporate interest in *"intellectual capital"* and *"knowledge management"* reflects a growing concern about identifying and exploiting information as a source of wealth creation and comparative advantage. Groupware connectivity, database mining, and report-generation software are examples of current efforts in this market for *"information capital."* However, these efforts focus upon information access, not **Information Capital Development (ICD).** In other words, it is assumed that the present information in our systems is of *"capital"* value and that we just need to access it. In reality, the marketplace has a great void in its current understanding of how to define and create valuable *"information capital."*

More managers and employees are responsible for creating and managing more and better information today than at any other time in history. This is a trend that is here to stay. Whether or not we choose to define our organizations as providers of information products or services, every organization is impacted by its ability to manage the use of information technologies. More important, every organization is impacted by its ability to manage the development of new and valuable information capital.

Future mechanical *breakthroughs* in micro-electronics aside, **IT** companies will contribute to "growing" the trillion-dollar market only by more broadly and deeply defining and addressing the information-capital requirements of the marketplace.

Information capital development, a critical source of wealth generation for every organization, allows us to continue building our **NCD Equation for Wealth Generation.** As the computer and telecommunication industries further converge upon a common mission— "the unimpeded flow of global information"—the equation for wealth generation is continually redefined (see Figure 8-4).

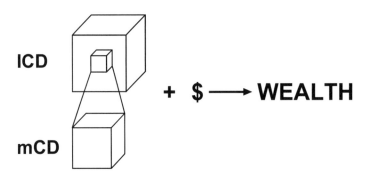

Figure 8-4. Wealth Driven by Information Capital

In the evolving Age of Ideation, the generation of information capital development replaces information resources as a source of wealth and competitive advantage. Together, information capital development and mechanical capital development become interdependent and synergistic, with each continuously redefined by its contributions to generating wealth. In an economic system powered by **ICD** technologies, information capital emerges as a *driving* ingredient in the generation of wealth.

Human Capital Development

The human-technology marketplace is the market of products and services that support and enable **Human Capital Development (HCD).** Thus far, our economies have focused upon mechanical and information technologies, and have grown in imbalance with our efforts to develop our human resources. **Human Technologies (HT)** are an emerging source of growth and comparative advantage (see Figure 8-5).

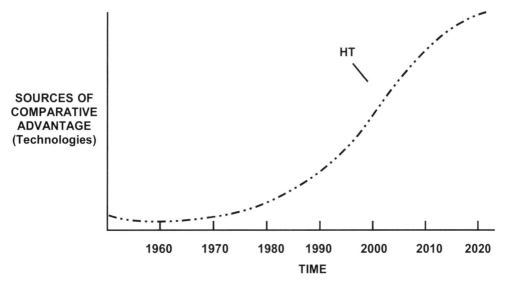

Figure 8-5. Market Impact of Human Technologies (HT)

The markets of human resource development, or education and training, represent more than one-half trillion dollars in the United States and are growing at the rate of nearly 10 percent per year. Although these huge markets are half the size of the trillion-dollar **IT** marketplace, we must remember one thing: it is *human performance* that develops information and mechanical products and services. Until we actualize the generative and innovative capabilities of our human capital, we will not actualize the potential contributions of information or machinery for wealth creation.

The business sector's growing interest in *"human capital"* and *"core competencies"* testifies to an increasing need to understand the ingredients of effective human performance. For businesses today, the **HCD** market-place strategies are a mix of technical training and "soft-skills" training. **"Soft skills"** are identifiable as multiple variations of basic interpersonal-communication skills. Generally, these skills are considered today's current *"human technologies."* However, the future skills requirements for human capital development are primarily intellectual skills that empower genera-tivity and innovativeness.

By choosing to define our organizations as human-technology businesses, and offering education, training, consulting services, or related software or media products, we are choosing to position ourselves in a now-accelerating commercial market curve. Requirements to elevate human performance have created a growth market. With an increased understanding of the factors that leverage human performance, companies will grow this **HCD** marketplace, empowering more and more people as sources of comparative advantage. It is critical that we understand and apply a new set of human technologies — methods to develop generative and innovative human performers.

Whether or not we choose to define our organizations as providers of **HCD** products or services, every organization is impacted by its ability to define and apply human technologies. Most important, every organization is impacted by its ability to empower and support innovative human perform-ance. Employees who can think are of growing value. Managers and employ-ees at every organizational level have a great need to understand and apply human technologies for human capital development.

HCD technologies and methods are a crucial source of wealth generation for us and our organizations. With them, we may further build our **NCD Equation for Wealth Generation.** As *breakthroughs* in human technologies occur, the equation continues to be redefined (see Figure 8-6).

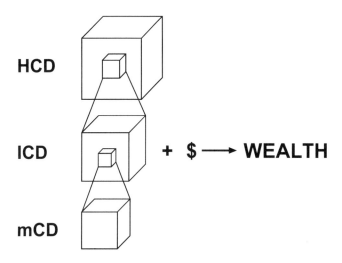

HCD

ICD   + $ ⟶ **WEALTH**

mCD

Figure 8-6. Wealth Driven by Human Capital

In the evolving Age of Ideation, human resources are redefined as innovative human processors, or human capital. Together, **HCD, ICD,** and **mCD** become interdependent and synergistic: each is continuously redefined by its contributions to generating wealth.

In an economic system powered by **HCD** technologies, human capital emerges as a *driving* economic ingredient. In synergistic relationship with information capital, human capital is capable of creating entirely new ingredients of wealth generation.

Organizational Capital Development

The organizational-technology marketplace is the market for organizational architecture and alignment services and support products. **Organizational Technologies (OT)** are another emerging source of growth and comparative advantage, as we can clearly see in Figure 8-7.

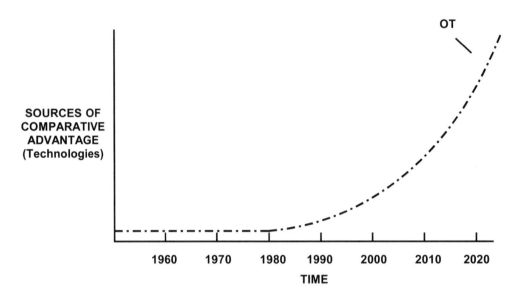

Figure 8-7. Market Impact of Organizational Technologies (OT)

With the "information overload" produced by information technologies, we decentralized our corporate operations. The effects were two-edged. On the one hand, decentralization allowed new sources of growth to emerge naturalistically — primary among them, human and information sources. On the other hand, decentralization dismantled the organization as a powerful source of effect in its own right.

We may realize that all of our resources — including machines, information, and people — operate within the contexts of our organizations; yet, until we actualize the functional alignment of our organizations' operations, we will not actualize these wealth-generating resources.

The need for continuous organizational alignment, within and between organizations, is ubiquitous. It is estimated that we are already spending five percent of **GDP** on internal restructuring annually: this would put the market estimate in the United States at over one-quarter trillion dollars and growing. In a changeable marketplace, every viable organization will engage in continuous organizational alignment throughout the 21st century. The commercial market for organizational alignment services and support products is a growth market.

Recent corporate interest in the *"reengineering"* of processes and the *"quality function deployment" (QFD)* of resources — as well as in *"self-organizing systems"* and *"flat," "matrixed," "virtual,"* and *"learning"* organizations — reflects a recognition that the organization itself requires attention as a valuable source of effect. The idea of the organization as a *"productive agency"* has reemerged. However, the aforementioned strategies of organizational architecture have already "played out." Corporate consultants and executives are now asking, "What's next?"

The market requires that organizational technologies serve both internal and external alignment. Organizational methodologies are needed for the internal alignment of all of the organization's critical operations: its goals or intentions, its resources, and its processes. Organizational technologies also need to deliver operational processes for external alignment with suppliers, vendors, and customer organizations.

Organization Capital Development (OCD), a critical source of wealth for every organization, allows us to build on our **NCD Equation for Wealth Generation** in the 21st century. With *breakthroughs* in organizational technologies, our equation is further refined to include the impact of **OCD** technologies (see Figure 8-8).

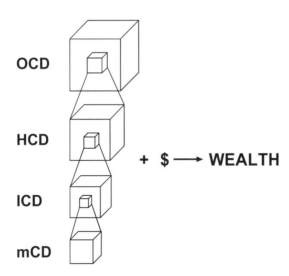

Figure 8-8. Wealth Driven by Organizational Capital

OCD technologies revitalize the organization by aligning the organization internally: its goals, resources, and processes. **OCD** technologies revitalize the organization with external-alignment strategies to align with suppliers and vendors as well as customers. This alignment defines organizational capital and results in the increased efficiency and effectiveness of what we call a *"possibilities organization."*

Marketplace Capital Development

Every organization is involved in making decisions about marketplace positioning and partnering. The market for positioning services to assist in these responsibilities is the market for marketplace technologies. Marketplace-positioning and -partnering methodologies enable producer organizations to strategically analyze and address their own marketplace requirements and values. These same technologies are also used to analyze the requirements and values of customers and competitors. **Marketplace Technologies (MT)** are the most powerful source of continuous growth and comparative advantage (see Figure 8-9).

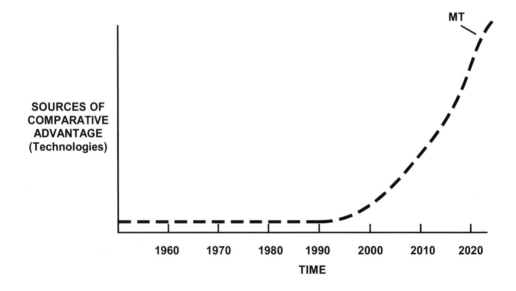

Figure 8-9. Market Impact of Marketplace Technologies (MT)

Most of us have already conceded that marketplace positioning is the prepotent source of corporate success. This, our greatest and most urgent corporate need, makes the marketplace-technology market a growth market.

Marketplace positioning is about positioning an organization in relation to other businesses in the marketplace. It implies aligning organizational divisions and units, positioning the talents of employees, positioning technologies, machinery, processes, and products and services, all in relation to counterparts in the economic marketplace.

Today, marketplace-positioning practices revolve around a few simple yet profound interrogatives:

- *"What business are you in?"*
- *"What business would you like to be in?"*
- *"How do you think you can make the transition?"*
- *"What are the obstacles?"*

Our current tools for marketplace positioning include market research, trend analysis, "what-if" scenario development, financial analyses, and industry best-practices benchmarking.

Requirements are imposed upon marketplace-positioning methods and practices: they must serve the policymaker's responsibilities regarding strategic decision-making and mergers and acquisitions; they must assist in making decisions about whether to enter a new market niche and whether to sell off a business line. Marketplace-positioning technologies can be defined as the *"how-to"* processes of marketplace positioning. Specifically, these technologies must help policymakers represent the values and capabilities of organizations and relate them to the requirements and opportunities of the marketplace. These technologies must walk policymakers through processes for positioning their organizations. With this in mind, we must ask ourselves whether our current marketplace-positioning strategies are adequate for the requirements of positioning our businesses for the next century.

MCD is a critical source of wealth for every organization. With the inclusion of **MCD** and marketplace technologies, our **NCD Equation for Wealth Generation** assumes a comprehensive form. The equation is further expanded to incorporate **MCD** technologies (see Figure 8-10).

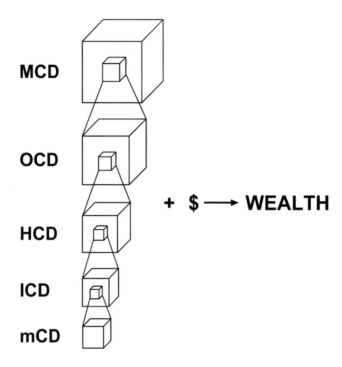

MCD

OCD

+ $ ⟶ WEALTH

HCD

ICD

mCD

Figure 8-10. Wealth Driven by Marketplace Capital

Policymakers are continuously processing the positioning of their organizations to maximize meeting and exceeding both current and future marketplace requirements.

NCD Equation for Wealth Generation

In our **NCD Equation for Wealth Generation** (shown in Figure 8-11), financial capital is reduced to a catalytic ingredient—necessary but not sufficient for capital development.

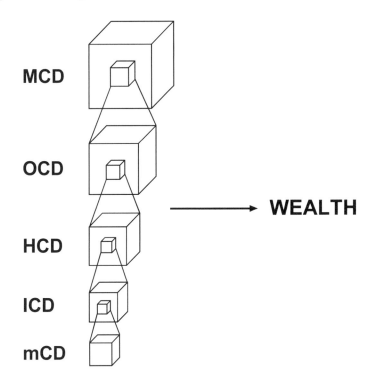

Figure 8-11. NCD Equation for Wealth Generation

As accounting procedures for *keeping score,* finances may appear on either side of the equation. Finances are used to invest in capital resource development and are used to measure the value of the many criteria of wealth. The new reality of ever-expanding wealth is generated by the ingredients of new capital development.

The all-important question is **"How?"** How can we accomplish the expanded version of **The Freedom Functions?**

- **Interdependent Cultural Relating** or interdependent relating between cultures;

- **Free Enterprise Economics** or entrepreneurially-driven free enterprise economics;

- **Direct Democratic Governance** or direct and representative democratic governance.

The Freedom Functions are the outcomes to which **The Freedom Doctrine** is dedicated. We will comment further upon the expanded version of **The Freedom Functions** in the chapters that follow.

The answer lies in **The NCD Components:**

- **MCD,** or positioning to differentiate the uniqueness of our products, services, and solutions in the marketplace;

- **OCD,** or organizational alignment of resources to implement marketplace positioning;

- **HCD,** or human empowerment in processing to implement organizational alignment;

- **ICD,** or information modeling to implement human processing;

- **mCD,** or mechanical tooling to implement information modeling.

Indeed, **The NCD Components** are **The Freedom Components that are dedicated to achieving The Freedom Functions.**

Without **NCD,** the accomplishment of **The Freedom Functions** is not possible. With **NCD,** the achievement of **The Freedom Functions** is imminently probable. **NCD** is a necessary but not sufficient condition of **The Freedom Functions.**

To sum, only through the development of all forms of new capital can we achieve lasting, peaceful, prosperous, and democratic societies. In economics as in life, the medium is the message: *only through the systematic development of our new capital resources can we achieve the freedom that empowers us to further develop our resources!*

References

Carkhuff, R. R. *The Age of the New Capitalism.* Amherst, MA: HRD Press, 1988.

Carkhuff, R. R. and Berenson, B. G. *The New Science of Possibilities. Volumes I and II.* Amherst, MA: HRD Press, 2000.

Carkhuff, R. R. and Berenson, B. G. *The Possibilities Organization.* Amherst, MA: HRD Press, 2000.

Carkhuff, R. R. and Berenson, B. G. *The Possibilities Economics.* Amherst, MA: HRD Press, 2002.

Carkhuff, R. R., Berenson, B. G. and Griffin, A. H. *The Possibilities Culture.* Amherst, MA: HRD Press, 2002.

Carkhuff, R. R., Carkhuff, C. J., and Cohen, B. *IP5D – Integrated Process Development: The Possibilities Business in the Possibilities Economy.* Amherst, MA: HRD Press, 2002.

Carkhuff, R. R., Carkhuff, C. J. and Kelly, J. T. *The GICCA Curve: The Possibilities Marketplace.* Amherst, MA: HRD Press, 2002.

Carkhuff, R. R., Griffin, A. H. and Berenson, B. G. *The Possibilities Community.* Amherst, MA: HRD Press, 2002.

O'Driscoll, G. P., Feulner, E. J., and O'Grady, M. A. *2003 Index of Economic Freedom.* Washington, DC: Heritage Foundation, 2003.

9. The Possibilities Culture

by Al Douds, M.S.W.
Sharon Fisher, M.Ed.
Richard M. Pierce, Ph.D.
Dennis Stanley, M.A.

The Possibilities Culture

MEANING

The Possibilities Culture is a culture of free, generative people. Developmentally, it is free and generative people who create a culture of possibilities. Yet, how can we build *The Possibilities Culture*?

An understanding of the culture of an individual and the context within which the individual lives, learns, and works, can help us understand the cultures of groups of people—families, communities, and nations.

In this chapter we learn about how to process values against contextual requirements. We will see that cultures, just like individuals, can measure their freedom by their methods for identifying their values and the contextual requirements within which they live, learn and work.

Culture-building is an ongoing responsibility of free people.

Dr. Andrew H. Griffin conducts "Ethnic Think Tanks" *with people of all cultures and subcultures. He begins with cultural pictures such as the following:*

> *Black infants, selected at random in the rural south, yield a developmental IQ of 117, approaching the superior range and reflecting a superior nervous system, which is the basis for intelligence. They are on the high margin of intelligence when compared to a mean IQ of 100. Yet with the inability of their protectors — their parents and their subcultures — to facilitate the development of their intelligence, by the time they are school age, they are already marginally low in intelligence, functioning in the 80 IQ range, which is borderline defective (Carkhuff, 1981, p. 138).*

Griffin asks the question: "Is there such a thing as a retarding culture?"
Moreover, he asks the critical question: "Can we reverse the effects of retarding cultures?" *And then he answers it!*

> *Taking the infants of borderline defective mothers (80 IQ range), helpers teach the mothers how to stimulate and respond to the children. At school age, the children of the mothers in the experimental group had IQs 25 to 30 points greater than the children in the control group, who had the predicted 80 IQs that are resultant from being left alone to be reared as they would ordinarily be reared (Carkhuff, 1981, p. 138).*

Griffin asks again: "Is there such a thing as a facilitative culture?" *The answer is a resounding* "Yes!"

The story presents a picture of two cultures — one facilitative and one retarding of human development. Griffin employs this picture as an entry learning experience to the study of **"Possibilities Culture"** *and* **"Probabilities Culture."** *It all begins with relating and enabling objectives:*

1. *To determine the level at which people want to relate within, between, and among cultures;*

2. *To determine the level at which people want to engage in economic enterprise in order to support their desired level of cultural relating;*

3. *To determine the level at which people want their governance to empower their desired levels of economic enterprise and cultural relating.*

In other words, Griffin models cultural self-determination by relating to people's frames of reference: for themselves and their families, for their schools and churches and neighborhoods, for their businesses and governance and communities.

Most people have no difficulty discriminating independence as their relating goal: they see no contradiction in terms. They understand the sad implications of dependency. They do not yet understand the happy implications of interdependency. Their only conflict comes when they determine the functions to which they would dedicate their independence: competition or collaboration with others.

The big question is the question of economic enterprise. What kind of economic system do they choose in order to achieve their desired level of relating? Here they understand the sad implications of welfare dependency. They understand the need to engage in economic enterprise either in the private sector or in the public sector. They know that economic enterprise is a necessary condition for the independence that they seek. They do not yet know the rewards of entrepreneurial initiative in a free enterprise system.

Finally, they answer the enabling question: what kind of governance do they need to engage in economic enterprise in order to learn to become independent? Here they recognize that they have been the passive victims of authoritarianism for all kinds of "isms": classism, racism, sexism, ageism, culturalism. They are increasingly motivated to participate in their own political destinies: at a minimum, to have input into the governance that determines many aspects of their lives; at a maximum, to join together to become forces for good. Collectively, they have no idea of the benefits of governance in supporting economic enterprise and relating: they cannot yet see governance and community as the generating engine that powers economics and relating.

In short, our profile of our people is a sad one, albeit hopeful. They seek independence; they choose economic enterprise of any kind; they select increased involvement in their own governance.

Come to think about it, they are not much different than the so-called "Third World" cultures that are scrambling for participation in the increasingly globalized and democratized free-enterprise global marketplace. They want to join the "global village" and trade in its marketplace. They seek the means to do so.

In this context, we may now illustrate cultural relating between nations:

Cultural Rep:	The truth of the matter is that we hate you because, with all your advances, you leave us farther and farther behind.
Freedom-Builder:	You're feeling helpless in the face of our advances.
Cultural Rep:	We hate your stock market, your Internet, your technological breakthroughs. Everything!
Freedom-Builder:	The more we move on, the more helpless you feel.
Cultural Rep:	To us, globalization means *"The Western way"*! You model it, but you don't give us a taste of it.
Freedom-Builder:	You feel cheated because we don't look back to share and help.
Cultural Rep:	Mostly, you don't look back to understand us. You just put it out there and say, "There it is — go for it!"
Freedom-Builder:	That is *"The Western way"*!
Cultural Rep:	But it is not *"The Eastern way"*! Nor any other way!
Freedom-Builder:	So you're furious because we create the models of progress, but we don't reach back to help others to develop their own unique versions of progress.
Cultural Rep:	Certainly, you have modeled independence and competitiveness. But you have only "mouthed" interdependence and collaboration.
Freedom-Builder:	You're saying, "We have talked the talk, but we have not walked the walk!"
Cultural Rep:	We cannot define a global village without living in it!
Freedom-Builder:	You're saying that we have failed because we have gone on without reference to real people in real time.

Cultural Rep: America, the great visionary of the global society, must now learn the lessons of its own creation: that there are extraordinary costs as well as benefits in the global marketplace.

Freedom-Builder: I accept your lessons. Mutual growth demands attention from all peoples to requirements as well as values.

Cultural Rep: Yes, but you have the luxury of setting the global requirements. What about our values?

Freedom-Builder: You're saying that if we hope to bring the world into a global marketplace, then we must introduce hope with empathic relating.

Cultural Rep: You have yet to understand the threat of hopelessness!

Freedom-Builder: If we are to advance global civilization, then we must make a long-term commitment to empathic relating…

Cultural Rep: …And action to reduce the fears of any people.

Freedom-Builder: While we have established the basis for a global village and pointed to its benefits in the global marketplace, we must now understand that its costs include both intentional action and profound levels of empathy.

Cultural Rep: Those are the costs of the global society. They are also the requirements for America and the Western World to help rebuild our nations.

Freedom-Builder: They are also the requirements for the Western World to come of age…

Cultural Rep: …And bring about the global village it so brilliantly envisioned.

Globalization has been represented by friend and foe alike as *"the march of international capitalism."*

> To its fiercest critics, globalization, the march of international capitalism, is a force for oppression, exploitation, and injustice. (*The Economist,* September 29, 2000, p. 3)

According to Carkhuff and Berenson, the problem with globalization is its definition in the probabilistic terms of our current economic systems. *Probabilities economics* assumes the normal distribution or variability of economic phenomena around some artifactual estimate of central tendency, and in so doing, it loses extraordinary phenomenal variability in so-called *"error variance."* Consequently, in imposing international economic integration upon economies, probabilities economics is *clueless* as to the uniqueness of both the individuals and the cultures involved. This leads, inevitably, to the attenuation of globalization.

The solution to globalization may be found in possibilistic terms. *Possibilities economics* assumes the individual differences of phenomenal performances: they are as uniquely unequal, multidimensional, interdependent, asymmetrical, curvilinear, and changeable as the tens of trillions of individual decisions made in the marketplace each day. Possibilities foster the individual and cultural relating systems that will lead, inevitably, to the actualization of globalization.

Carkhuff and Berenson view the probabilistic and possibilistic systems in sharp relief in Table 9-1, which defines their critical assumptions, implications, and processes. As we may note, the probabilities course defines globalization in economic terms as the economic integration of markets. The direct implication is that those economies that promote capitalism and free trade will prosper. The implied processes are that all economies must accept international capitalism as the ultimate form of economic enterprise.

Table 9-1.
Assumptions, Implications, and Processes of Globalization

	Probabilities Course	Possibilities Course
Assumptions	Globalization is defined by *"international capitalism"*; e.g., the economic integration of markets.	Globalization is defined by *"cultural relating"*; e.g., the level of relationships between cultures in the global society.
Implications	Those economies that promote capitalism and free trade will prosper.	Those cultures that dedicate economic and governance initiatives to cultural relating will prosper.
Processes	All economies must accept international capitalism as the ultimate form of economic enterprise.	All cultures can make self-determinations concerning their levels of cultural relating, economies, and governance.

The possibilistic course, in turn, defines globalization in cultural terms as *"cultural relating"*; e.g., the degree to which cultures aspire to relate to other cultures in the global society. The implications may be viewed in systems terms: those cultures that dedicate their economic and governance enterprises to cultural relating will succeed and prosper. The explicit processes are that all cultures can make self-determinations concerning their levels of desired cultural relating as well as their modes of enabling economics and governance.

The probabilities and possibilities courses contrast vividly in terms of the level of client self-determination. The probabilities course requires the acceptance of international capitalism. The possibilities course offers the client culture the benefits of self-determination.

Of course, it follows, for example, that when a client culture has selected to relate independently and competitively with other cultures, it must select the best available economic and governance systems to enable it to do so. That is the nature of self-determination. It is also the nature of discovery learning!

Possibilities Economics

Whereas probabilities economics assumes *"capitalism makes the world go 'round,"* possibilities economics assumes that *"markets make the world go 'round."* In that context, Carkhuff and Berenson define globalization as cultural relating in the marketplace: all cultures can make self-determinations concerning the levels of relating, economics, and governance to which they aspire. The following points are essential to their view.

1. Globalization begins with cultural relating.

Globalization is about relating—cultural relating. Like neighbors in a village, people must first determine the degree to which they desire to relate. We may scale relating any way we choose because it reflects our values. However, we must also scale relating in terms of the requirements that the marketplace imposes upon our village. For example, we may scale relating in terms of the requirements for commerce in our village, as shown in Table 9-2. As we may see, the levels range from dependence to interdependence.

Table 9-2. Levels of Cultural Relating

LEVELS	CULTURAL RELATING
5	Interdependence
4	Collaborative
3	Independence
2	Competitive
1	Dependence

At the lower levels, people are dependent and reactive. At the higher levels, people are interdependent and initiative. Most people aspire to some level of independence. Some dedicate this independence to competing.

Others dedicate their independence to collaborating. Indeed, it is because they have an independent contribution to make that they can collaborate and, perhaps with maturity, relate interdependently.

2.   Relating is accomplished by economics.

Like neighbors in a village bazaar, people are brought into intimacy when they relate as producer and consumer or seller and buyer. Again, while we may scale economics in any manner to reflect our values, we must be aware of the requirements for commerce that will enable us to achieve our relating level. For example, we may scale economics in terms of the requirements for accomplishing our relating goals, as shown in Table 9-3. As we may see, the levels range from control to free enterprise.

At the lower levels, people employ controlled economies, while at the higher levels, people use free-enterprise-driven economies to accomplish their cultural relating goals. Most people aspire to at least some level of a mixed economy: capitalistic for profitability; command-driven for regulation. Depending upon their success in achieving their goals, people may opt to become increasingly one or the other: capitalistic or command. Indeed, it is because they have a mixed economy that they can choose—continuously—to align with their relating goals.

Table 9-3. Levels of Economics

LEVELS	ECONOMICS
5	Free Enterprise
4	Capitalistic
3	Mixed
2	Command
1	Control

3. Economics is enabled by governance.

Like neighbors in a village meeting, people become citizens when they promote their ideas. Again, while we may scale governance in any manner to reflect our values, we must be aware of the requirements for governance that will enable us to empower our economics and achieve our relating goals. For example, we may scale governance in terms of the requirements for enabling economics, as shown in Table 9-4. As we may see, the levels range from totalitarian to free democratic.

Table 9-4. Levels of Governance

LEVELS	GOVERNANCE
5	Free Democratic
4	Representative
3	Mixed
2	Authoritarian
1	Totalitarian

At lower levels, people employ totalitarian governance, while at higher levels, people use free democratic-driven governance to accomplish the economic empowerment goals. Most people aspire at least to some level of mixed governance: representative for opportunity; authoritarian for security. Depending upon their success in achieving their goals, people may opt to become increasingly one or the other: democratic or authoritarian. Again, it is because they have been exposed to a mixed economy that they can choose — continuously — to align with their economic and relating goals.

4. Globalization is defined by cultural relating, economic enterprise, and governance.

Just as with neighbors in a village, then, cultural relating is integrated with economics and governance. If we employ these scaled dimensions in a 3D model, such as shown in Figure 9-1, we may see how the different levels of the different dimensions themselves relate. For example, we may see that high levels of relating cannot be accomplished by low levels of economics and governance. Likewise, we may conclude that mixed models for governance and economics yield mixed results for relating. In short, globalization is **Cultural Capital Development, or CCD'.**

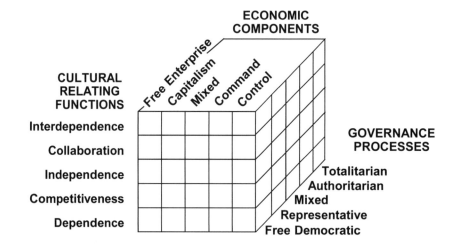

Figure 9-1. Cultural Capital Development Model

5. *The Possibilities Culture* **is actualized at the highest levels of Cultural Capital Development.**

In this context, we may begin to realize that cultural relating is actualized only with the highest levels of economic enterprise and governance. We may select the cube with the highest levels of all **CCD'** scales: interdependent cultural relating, free enterprise economics, free democratic governance (see Figure 9-2). This cube represents *The Possibilities Culture.* Policies based upon this possibilities cube will yield the highest levels of benefits on all measurable indices: performance, production, productivity, profitability, growth. We may define it as follows:

Interdependent cultural relating is accomplished by free enterprise economics enabled by free democratic governance.

In short, cultural relating is the mission of **Cultural Capital Development.**

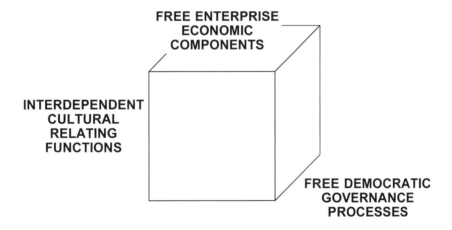

Figure 9-2. The Possibilities Culture

6. *The Possibilities Economics* **is actualized at the highest levels of Economic Capital Development, or ECD.**

As shown in Figure 9-3, the governance capital development **(GCD)** components and the community capital development **(CCD)** processes are aligned to accomplish economic capital development **(ECD)**. At the highest levels, *The Possibilities Economics* is defined by **ECD:**

> *Free enterprise economics are achieved by free democratic governance enabled by generative community processes.*

In short, **Economic Capital Development** is the vehicle for accomplishing **Cultural Capital Development.**

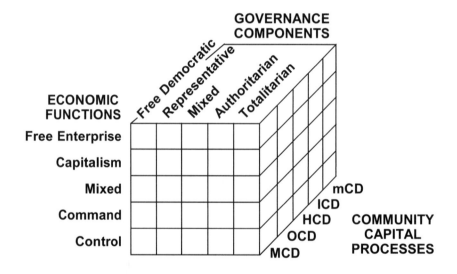

Figure 9-3. Economic Capital Development Model

7. *The Possibilities Governance* **is actualized at the highest levels of Governance Capital Development, or GCD.**

As shown in Figure 9-4, the community capital development **(CCD)** components and the new capital development **(NCD)** processes are aligned to accomplish governance capital development **(GCD).** At the highest levels, *The Possibilities Governance* is defined by **GCD:**

> *Free democratic governance accomplished by* **NCD** *– generating communities enabled by new capital development, or* **NCD.**

In short, **Governance Capital Development** is the empowering, enabling system for **Economic Capital Development** and **Cultural Capital Development.**

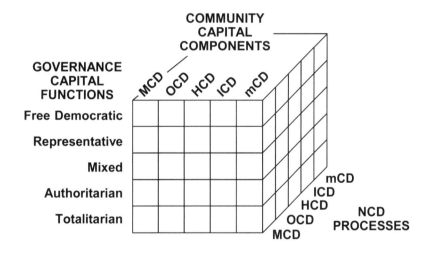

Figure 9-4. Governance Capital Development Model

Interdependent Relating Cultures

For Carkhuff and Berenson, all cultures are composed of communities (see Figure 9-5). In this context, all cultures relate or not. In the illustration, the cultures are depicted as relating interdependently between and among communities. As defined by *"mutual processing for mutual benefit,"* interdependent relating such as this is rare. Nevertheless, like a good marriage, it is held up as the model for exemplary relating: the cultures process interdependently for their mutual benefits.

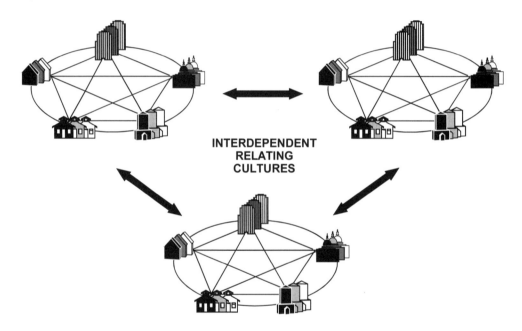

**INTERDEPENDENT
RELATING
CULTURES**

Figure 9-5. Cultural Capital Development

Clearly, cultures can and do have good relationships at other levels. Certainly, for example, independent cultures dedicated to collaborating are recipients of mutual benefit. The discriminating dimension between collaboration and interdependency is processing: interdependently related cultures process together without knowing beforehand what the outcomes will be.

Can other cultures benefit from other levels of relating? Absolutely! That is what currently makes the world go 'round: independent cultures dedicated to competitive relating in the marketplace. When there is a match between the producers' products and the consumers' needs, then there may be contracts for mutual benefits as buyers and sellers negotiate a price.

Unfortunately, at the lowest level of relating, dependency, there are limited benefits. When cultures relate only dependently, they tend to derive few benefits from their contracts because they have no leverage in negotiating. Consequently, they tend to become reactive and even hostile to the cultures that serve them and even support them.

For Carkhuff and Berenson, the test of cultural capital development is in the doing. We test our principles by practicing them. We test our hypotheses by evaluating our performance. We modify our principles with the changes in our performance. *The Possibilities Culture* is about generating these changes: new and better ways of relating, of conducting commerce, of practicing government.

In transition, Carkhuff and Berenson conclude that globalization is defined by the level of cultural relating discharged by the level of economic enterprise, which is enabled by the level of governance. It begins and ends with relating—continuous relating—within, between, and among cultures. We may now illustrate building *The Possibilities Culture* by returning to our "Cultural Representative" and "Freedom-Builder."

Culture Rep:	The big decision that we must make is to attempt to maximize meeting both our cultural values and the evolving cultural requirements.
Freedom-Builder:	That is a profound moment!
Cultural Rep:	A possibilities moment!
Freedom-Builder:	We began by expanding our alternatives.
Cultural Rep:	We are now ready to narrow our options.
Freedom-Builder:	Let's begin by taking a look at our cultural relating values.

Cultural Rep: I believe that we are currently relating dependently and reactively and that we need to learn to relate independently and competitively. [See Figure 9-6.]

Freedom-Builder: In other words, your dependency values enable you only to meet dependency requirements.

Cultural Rep: Dependency is unsatisfactory. We need to learn to relate independently.

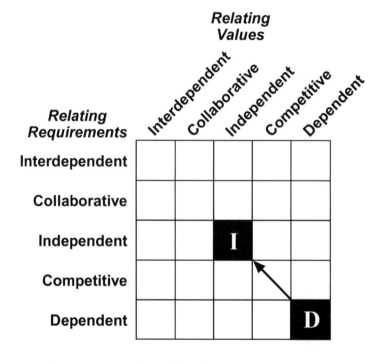

Figure 9-6. Cultural Relating Requirements
and Values

Freedom-Builder: Independence gives you choices that you do not now have.

Cultural Rep: Yes! In some areas, we need to be competitive. Maybe later we will want to be collaborative.

Freedom-Builder: This is a most difficult leap forward. You must elevate two spaces. You must proceed developmentally in a manner that you can manage. What about economic enterprise?

Cultural Rep: I believe that we are currently in a command economy and that we must learn to free our economic initiative in a mixed economy. [See Figure 9-7.]

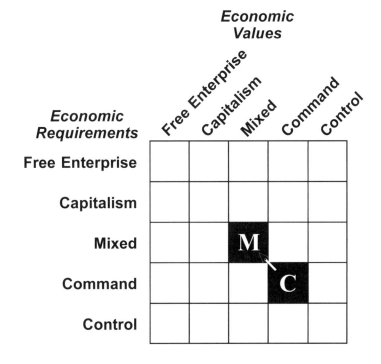

Figure 9-7. Economic Requirements and Values

Freedom-Builder: In other words, your command and control values enable you only to meet command requirements.

Cultural Rep: And that, too, is most unsatisfactory.

Freedom-Builder: Again, the mixed economy gives you choices that you do not now have.

Cultural Rep: Yes! We can continue to participate with some command economic policies while beginning to explore capitalism.

Freedom-Builder: This appears to be a manageable development goal. What about governance?

Cultural Rep: I believe that we currently have authoritarian governance and that we must aspire to a mixed form of governance. [See Figure 9-8.]

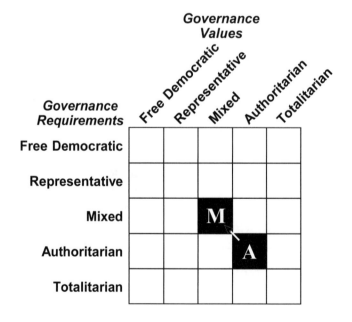

Figure 9-8. Governance Requirements and Values

Freedom-Builder: In other words, your authoritarian values enable you only to meet authoritarian requirements.

Cultural Rep: Again, unsatisfactory. Only the mixed governance will give us a balance of freedom and authority.

Freedom-Builder: This goal is manageable. So what will your new image of cultural capital development look like?

Cultural Rep: Independent cultural relating functions will be accomplished by mixed economic components enabled by mixed governance processes. [See Figure 9-9.]

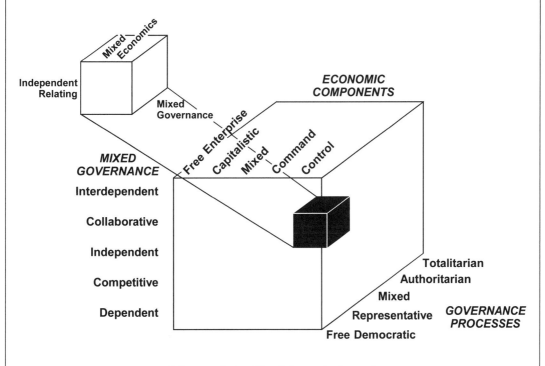

Figure 9-9. The New Cultural Capital Development Model

Freedom-Builder:	That's really exciting because it gives us all hope.
Cultural Rep:	It's fulfilling because it provides us with a model to guide our own destiny.
Freedom-Builder:	If you are fulfilled, then we are fulfilled.
Cultural Rep:	I never thought we would think in these futuristic terms. What about your culture?
Freedom-Builder:	Our culture has to keep moving in order to help your culture keep moving.
Cultural Rep:	We all must change simultaneously ...
Freedom-Builder:	And hopefully, interdependently!

In conclusion, let us return to Dr. Griffin and his *"Ethnic Think Tanks."* In these think tanks, Griffin deals with the necessity of economic systems to accomplish relating goals. At a global level, he also invites the movement toward the free enterprise marketplace as a precondition of all relating. Just as individuals, families, and subcultures in the community must dedicate their economic enterprise to their desired levels of cultural relating, so must nations dedicate their free market enterprise to collaborative or interdependent relating.

For Griffin, the spiraling changes in the global marketplace have converged to define the inevitability of the free market: technological changes, particularly in transportation and communication; information changes, especially in the transmission of innovations in products and services; the flow of trade, investment, and capital across historic borders. Above all else, Griffin emphasizes the communication of ideas across historic borders: ***"Big Ideas!"*** In short, globalization means that different cultures have overcome the obstacles of boundaries to become a *"connected"* world.

In this context, Griffin stresses the contributions of governance and the community towards empowering or enabling the economic system to accomplish the desired level of cultural relating. Together, governance and the community are the generating engine that powers the economic and cultural systems. They generate the required new capital: marketplace, organization, human, information, and mechanical. They produce the enlightened citizens, the progressive leaders, the productive workers, and the transcultural relators that enable the other systems to go and grow.

Just as with Griffin's *"Ethnic Think Tanks,"* all healthy people in all healthy cultures must choose the levels of culture to which they aspire: relating ranging to collaborating and interdependency; economic enterprise ranging to entrepreneurial-driven, free enterprise; governance ranging to free and direct democratic participation. These are the cultural objectives of the 21st century global village and its marketplace. When we choose for our cultures, we choose for our children!

The storyboards with which Griffin initiated his entry learning experiences in the *"Ethnic Think Tanks"* are real. They tell the story of two cultures: one bound in cultural nonresponsiveness and isolation; the other freed by personalized responsiveness and individualized initiative in relating. The two cultures yield very different outcomes for their children: one produces dependent and reactive *"infantile"* children; the other generates interdependent and generative mature adults.

In their maturity or immaturity, one culture will live within itself, entropically exhausting its own resources; the other will live in an integrated world, heuristically multiplying its resources and their benefits.

One is a retarding culture and ultimately produces socially and intellectually retarded people. The other is a facilitative culture and continuously generates socially and intellectually facilitative people.

One is *"The Probabilities Culture,"* where there is no way out from the condemning assumptions of *"normality"* and *"linearity"* and *"hard-wired"* conditioning.

The other is **The Possibilities Culture,** where our potentially infinite and unique brainpower generates potentially infinite possibilities for ourselves and our neighbors.

It all begins with relating!

References

Carkhuff, R. R. *Toward Actualizing Human Potential.* Amherst, MA: HRD Press, 1981.

Carkhuff, R. R. and Berenson, B. G. *The Possibilities Economics.* Amherst, MA: HRD Press, 2002.

Carkhuff, R. R., Berenson, B. G. and Griffin, A. H. *The Possibilities Culture.* Amherst, MA: HRD Press, 2002.

Carkhuff, R. R., Griffin, A. H. and Berenson, B. G. *The Possibilities Community.* Amherst, MA: HRD Press, 2002.

Griffin, A. H. *The Multi-Ethnic Think Tank: Position Statements.* Olympia, WA: Office of Superintendent of Public Instruction, State of Washington, 2001.

Griffin, A. H. *The Unity Project.* Olympia, WA: Office of Superintendent of Public Instruction, State of Washington, 2001.

10. The Possibilities Nation
by Robert R. Carkhuff, Ph.D.
Alja Knezevic, M.Ed.
Ratko Knezevic, M.A.
Rob Owen, M.B.A.

The Possibilities Nation

MEANING

The Possibilities Nation is a nation of free people. Developmentally, free people join together to create ***The Possibilities Nation***.

A truism of performance is "you get what you measure for." If a nation does not define national performance it will not know when it has reached its goals. Freedom requires performance measures to orient us and challenge us.

This chapter presents 5 inter-related scales for measuring freedom: a cultural relating scale, a scale for economic performance, a governmental action scale, ***The New Capital Development Scale***, as well as an overarching ***Leader-through-Detractor Scale***. These practical tools can help us measure our nation's freedom and its movement toward becoming ***The Possibilities Nation***.

It all began with a visit from the prospective president of a Third World country and his associates. We began the session by asking the following questions of these clients:

> • *"What is your current image of your country?"*
> • *"What is your future vision for your country?"*

Our clients responded by relating a story about the history and the politics of the country, to which we responded:

> *"You are rightfully proud of the human soul of your country – its energy, its courage, its spirituality – but it has gone to sleep and you would like to wake it up."*

Having gotten their attention, we added:

> *"All that you have told us about your country's proud history sum-totals to less than one percent of its future!"*

By way of explanation, we added the historic principle of generativity:

> *"All futuristic visions dwarf the contributions of previous eras!"*

Put another way, traditions may be platforms that build us up or quagmires that take us down.

So it has been as humankind has moved from hunter-gatherers to agrarian civilizations; from agrarian to industrial eras; from industrial to information ages. So will it now be as we move from the Information Age to the **Age of Ideation.** Each new age reduces the contributions of the previous age exponentially: the previous ages become insufficient conditions for a vision of growth.

So it will also be as each nation develops a futuristic vision to join the global village and its marketplace. As conditions change, we become part of the change. Moreover, we intentionally initiate the change.

The clients responded:

> *"It is a relief to find someone who is confident in helping us look forward rather than backward."*

The Freedom-Building Vision

The *Freedom-Building* vision began with images of the levels of dimensions to which the clients aspired (see Table 10-1). Our clients processed before producing the following discriminations of scaled dimensions:

> • *Transitional independence dedicated, ultimately, to collaborative relations with neighboring cultures and nations;*
>
> • *Transitional capitalism dedicated, ultimately, to entrepreneurially driven, free economic enterprise;*
>
> • *Transitional representative governance dedicated, ultimately, to free and direct democracy.*

Table 10-1. The Freedom-Building Scales

LEVELS	CULTURAL RELATING— CCD′	ECONOMIC ENTERPRISE— ECD	GOVERNANCE SUPPORT— GCD	COMMUNITY DEVELOPMENT— CCD
Leader	Interdependent	Free Enterprise	Free and Direct	MCD
Contributor	Collaborative	Capitalistic	Representative	OCD
Participant	Independent	Mixed	Mixed	HCD
Subtractor	Competitive	Command	Authoritarian	ICD
Detractor	Dependent	Control	Totalitarian	mCD

We then transformed the discriminations of the mission into a dimensional model of the cultural capital development **(CCD′)** vision. This model is shown in Figure 10-1. As may be viewed, independent relating functions of **CCD′** are achieved (or discharged) by capitalistic economic components of economic capital development **(ECD)** enabled by representative democratic governance, or governance capital development **(GCD).** In other words, governance supports economics to achieve independence.

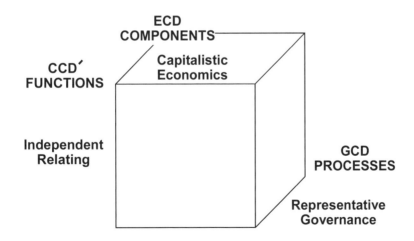

Figure 10-1. The Cultural Vision of Freedom-Building

The dimensionality of the vision communicated the interdependency of the *Freedom-Building* dimensions: culture, economics, governance. The dimensionality of the vision also defined the mission of *Freedom-Building:*

> **Clients:**
> *"We are happy to be able to view the interactions of the dimensions and to study the implications of these interactions."*

The Freedom-Building Mission

In this manner, the mission of *Freedom-Building* was defined by the vision of *Freedom-Building:*

> **Clients:**
> *"Transitionally independent cultural relating discharged by capitalistic economics enabled by representative democratic governance."*

This cultural mission led directly into the enabling economic mission.

In order to accomplish the cultural **(CCD')** mission, we needed to implement the economic **(ECD)** mission. This is illustrated in Figure 10-2. As we may see, the economic components of the cultural mission were rotated deductively (counter-clockwise) to become the capitalistic functions of the economic mission. In turn, governance was rotated to become the discharging components. Finally, marketplace positioning of the community capital development, or **CCD,** was introduced as the enabling processes.

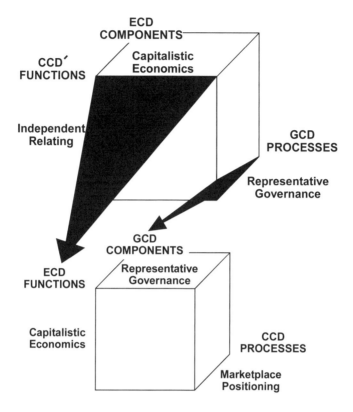

Figure 10-2. The Economic Vision of Freedom-Building

Marketplace positioning was introduced to enable representative governance to accomplish (or discharge) capitalistic economics. Such positioning means that the community must be positioned in the marketplace in order to generate the **NCD** required for governance to support economic enterprise.

> **Clients:**
> *"We are pleased to understand the roles of economic enterprise in fostering cultural relating and governance in supporting or enabling economic enterprise."*

Furthermore, in order to accomplish the economic **(ECD)** mission, we needed to implement the governance **(GCD)** mission. This is shown in Figure 10-3. As may be viewed, the governance components of the economic mission were rotated deductively to become the representative functions of the governance mission. In turn, the marketplace positioning of the community processes was rotated to become discharging components. Finally, organizational alignment was introduced as the enabling **NCD** processes.

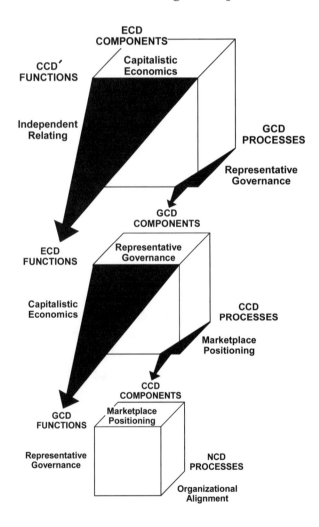

Figure 10-3. The Governance Vision of Freedom-Building

The organizational alignment served to introduce the **NCD** models that empower the community with new capital (see Figure 10-4):

- **MCD** — Marketplace Capital Development, or positioning,
- **OCD** — Organizational Capital Development, or alignment,
- **HCD** — Human Capital Development, or processing,
- **ICD** — Information Capital Development, or modeling,
- **mCD** — Mechanical Capital Development, or tooling.

As illustrated, each **NCD** model is rotated deductively to generate the empowering objectives of new capital development: **MCD > OCD > HCD > ICD > mCD.**

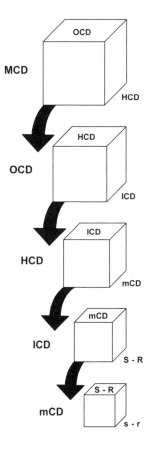

Figure 10-4. The NCD Models

In turn, this means that all of the **NCD** models need to be implemented in order to provide the new capital that the community requires. The community is the generating engine that empowers governance to support economic enterprise in achieving the targeted level of cultural relating in the 21st century global society.

> **Clients:**
> *"We are ecstatic to have an initial image of a vision. We understand that an operational definition makes the vision achievable."*

Freedom-Building Resources

The clients knew that it was not enough to define the benefits to which they aspired. They also had to define the resources or capacities that they would dedicate to achieving these benefits. *The Freedom-Building Matrix,* shown in Table 10-2, assisted them in this task. Here we find the resources or capacities that are dedicated to meeting the requirements of, and thus to achieving the benefits of, *Freedom-Building.*

As may be noted, requirements are defined by levels of cultural, economic, governance, and community capital development. Similarly, resources are defined by the same scaled resources. Ultimately, our levels of resources or capacities — existing, empowered, or acquired — will determine our success in accomplishing our desired levels of requirements and benefits.

Table 10-2. The Freedom-Building Matrix

REQUIREMENTS		RESOURCES			
		Cultural Capital Development 5 4 3 2 1	Economic Capital Development 5 4 3 2 1	Governance Capital Development 5 4 3 2 1	Community Capital Development 5 4 3 2 1
Cultural Capital Development	5 4 3 2 1	Cultural Relating Resources in service of Cultural Relating Requirements	Economic Enterprise Resources in service of Cultural Relating Requirements	Governance Support Resources in service of Cultural Relating Requirements	Community Generating in service of Cultural Relating Requirements
Economic Capital Development	5 4 3 2 1	Cultural Relating Resources in service of Economic Enterprise Requirements	Economic Enterprise Resources in service of Economic Enterprise Requirements	Governance Support Resources in service of Economic Enterprise Requirements	Community Generating in service of Economic Enterprise Requirements
Governance Capital Development	5 4 3 2 1	Cultural Relating Resources in service of Governance Support Requirements	Economic Enterprise Resources in service of Governance Support Requirements	Governance Support Resources in service of Governance Support Requirements	Community Generating in service of Governance Support Requirements
Community Capital Development	5 4 3 2 1	Cultural Relating Resources in service of Community Generating Requirements	Economic Enterprise Resources in service of Community Generating Requirements	Governance Support Resources in service of Community Generating Requirements	Community Generating in service of Community Generating Requirements

In the matrix, the requirements and resources were scaled so that the clients could determine the level of resources they needed in order to achieve the level of requirements they desired.

As we illustrated for our clients:

- If we target capitalistic economics, then we need resources to accomplish them — privatization and deregulation of enterprise and the like.

- Similarly, if we target representative democracy, then we need resources to accomplish this — enlightenment and empowerment of the citizenry and the like.

- Likewise, if we target new capital development, or **NCD,** by the generating engine of the community, then we require resources appropriate for accomplishing this.

The New Capital Development Matrix, in Table 10-3, furthers this illustration. Here we find producer resources or capabilities that are dedicated to meeting customer requirements and benefits. In general, **Infrastructure Building** concentrates upon the lower, more physical levels of **NCD** systems: mechanical and information capital development. Unfortunately, **Infrastructure Building** does not emphasize the **NCD** systems within which the lower forms of capital development operate: marketplace, organization, human. Moreover, **Infrastructure Building** does not emphasize the *Freedom-Building* systems within which all **NCD** systems are nested.

As may be noted, customer requirements are defined by levels of new capital development: **MCD, OCD, HCD, ICD, mCD.** Similarly, producer resources or capacities are defined by levels of **NCD** technological capabilities: **MT, OT, HT, IT, mT.** This means that we can determine the level of producer technological capabilities that we need in order to achieve the level of customer requirements we desire.

Table 10-3.
The New Capital Development Matrix

Producer Capabilities

Customer Requirements	Marketplace Technologies	Organizational Technologies	Human Technologies	Information Technologies	Mechanical Technologies
MCD - Marketplace Capital Development	Marketplace Positioning of Marketplace Capital	Marketplace Alignment Analysis	Policy Empowerment	Intranet/Internet Software	Internet Hardware
OCD - Organizational Capital Development	Marketplace Positioning of Organizational Capital	Organizational Alignment Analysis	Executive Empowerment	Groupware Software	Wide Area Network Hardware
HCD - Human Capital Development	Marketplace Positioning of Human Capital	Human Capital Alignment Analysis	Manager Empowerment	Decision Support Systems Software	Local Area Network Hardware
ICD - Information Capital Development	Marketplace Positioning of Information Capital	Information Alignment Analysis	Knowledge Worker Empowerment	Office Software	Computer
mCD - Mechanical Capital Development	Marketplace Positioning of Mechanical Capital	Machine Operations Alignment Analysis	Machine Operator Training	CAD-CAM Software	Machine Tool

For example:

- If we target **MCD** positioning at a highly differentiated level for comparative advantage, then we need high levels of the following technological capacities: marketplace positioning, marketplace alignment, policy empowerment, intranet/internet software, internet hardware.

- Similarly, if we target **OCD** at highly aligned levels, then we need high levels of the following technological capacities: organizational positioning, organizational alignment, executive empowerment, groupware software, wide-area-network hardware.

- Likewise, if we target **HCD** at highly generative levels, then we need high levels of the following technological capacities: human positioning, human alignment, management empowerment, decision support software, local-area-network hardware.

Again, all producer capabilities are dedicated to meeting desired customer benefits and their requirements.

Clients:
"We are really eager to get on with the designs to implement the vision. We believe strongly that education must be among the first of our targets."

This emphasis on education and subsequent processing with our clients provided us with the following case study in human capital development, or **HCD.**

HCD: A Case Study

Our clients were committed to developing human capital to accomplish the following functions:

> **Clients:**
> *"To enable community as the generating engine for all* **NCD:**
> - *To empower governance functions with an enlightened citizenry;*
> - *To implement economic functions with enterprising workers;*
> - *To actualize cultural functions with collaborative peoples."*

For the client nation, **HCD** meant schooling: defining the functions, components, and processes required for **HCD** in the 21st century global marketplace. Here is the model we designed together (Figure 10-5).

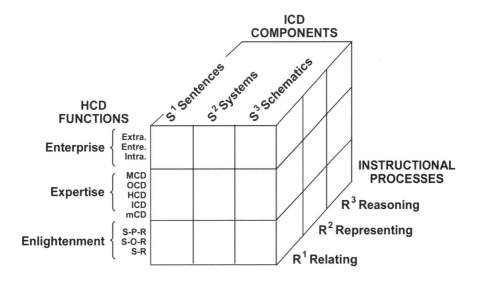

Figure 10-5. The Possibilities Schools Model

Note that the schooling functions emphasize preparation for enlightenment, expertise, and enterprise:

- **Enlightenment in Thinking Skills**
    - **S-R,** or conditioned responding
    - **S-O-R,** or discriminative learning
    - **S-P-R,** or generative thinking

- **Expertise in New Capital Development (NCD) Skills**
    - **MCD,** or marketplace positioning
    - **OCD,** or organizational alignment
    - **HCD,** or human processing
    - **ICD,** or information modeling
    - **mCD,** or mechanical tooling

- **Enterprise Skills**
    - Intrapreneurial
    - Entrepreneurial
    - Extrapreneurial

The school systems were designed to accomplish these results outputs (Figure 10-6). As may be viewed, levels of information capital constituted the resource inputs:

- S^1 — Sentence-based
- S^2 — Systems-based
- S^3 — Schematics-based

In turn, these resource inputs were transformed into our desired results outputs by instructional processes:

- R^1 — Relating,
- R^2 — Representing,
- R^3 — Reasoning.

All of the processes take place within facilitative contextual conditions:

- **Relating to human experience,**
- **Empowering of human potential,**
- **Freeing of empowered human potential.**

Finally, standards of excellence assess levels of performance:

- **Uniform measures of basic skills,**
- **Diverse measures of discriminating skills,**
- **Changeable measures of generating skills.**

We label these systems operations *"The New Possibilities Schools"* because they are able to generate new possibilities in all areas of human endeavor.

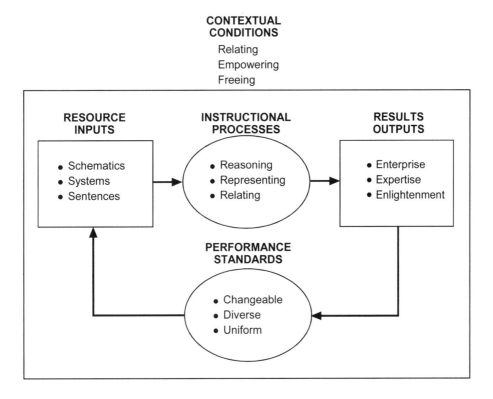

Figure 10-6. The New Possibilities Schools System

To summarize the above, the information resource inputs are transformed by the instructional processes *(The New 3Rs)* into desired results outputs. *The New Possibilities Schools* are capable of generating human capital that, in turn, is capable of generating all other forms of new capital.

In short, the learner products of schooling will be able to think creatively, initiate entrepreneurially, and implement with expertise. For example, the clients discovered that these thinking entrepreneurs know far more than simply how to develop websites on the Internet.

> **Clients:**
> *"These learner products know …*
> - *How to position their products or services in the marketplace (MCD);*
> - *How to align their organizations with the positioning (OCD);*
> - *How to empower the people with thinking to implement the alignment (HCD);*
> - *How to generate information models to implement the thinking (ICD);*
> - *How to produce mechanical tools to implement the modeling (mCD)."*

In other words, the enlightened entrepreneurs are empowered to participate in the global village and its marketplace.

The clients discovered that no other schools in the world prepare their youth to meet, exceed, and even *generate* these 21st century requirements. As our clients put it:

> **Clients:**
> *"Our new century requires …*
> - *Thinking and enlightened people,*
> - *Enterprising and entrepreneurial people,*
> - *Empowered and expert people."*

Elevated levels of **HCD** make everything else possible!

The clients also discovered that to join the global village and its marketplace, it takes three things:

> **Clients:**
> 1. *"Big ideas! Really big ideas about what is possible!"*
> 2. *"New technologies! Real technologies to implement the possible with the probable!"*
> 3. *"Enlightened leaders! Real commitments to follow through on the changes in all* **NCD** *and* **CCD'** *systems."*

These are keys to growth in 21st century *Freedom-Building!*
The clients now formulated the three pillars of their country's mission:

> **Clients:**
> - *"Independence achieved by enterprise!"*
> - *"Enterprise supported by democracy!"*
> - *"Democracy empowered by community!"*

Then they summarized:

> - *"Enterprise!"*
> - *"Democracy!"*
> - *"Community!"*

Finally, they formulated their personal vision:

> **Clients:**
> - *"To awaken the soul of a slumbering giant!"*
> - *"To build* **The Possibilities Nation!** *"*

References

Carkhuff, R. R. *The Age of the New Capitalism.* Amherst, MA: HRD Press, 1988.

Carkhuff, R. R. *Empowering.* Amherst, MA: HRD Press, 1989.

Carkhuff, R. R., and Berenson, B. G. *The Possibilities Economics.* Amherst, MA: HRD Press, 2002.

Carkhuff, R. R., Berenson, B. G., and Griffin, A. H. *The Possibilities Culture.* Amherst, MA: HRD Press, 2002.

Carkhuff, R. R., Carkhuff, C. J. and Cohen, B. *IP⁵D – Integrated Process Development: The Possibilities Business in the Possibilities Economy.* Amherst, MA: HRD Press, 2002.

Carkhuff, R. R., Carkhuff, C. J., and Kelly, J. T. *The GICCA Curve: The Possibilities Marketplace.* Amherst, MA: HRD Press, 2002.

Carkhuff, R. R., Griffin, A. H., and Berenson, B. G. *The Possibilities Community.* Amherst, MA: HRD Press, 2002.

Novak, M. *The Spirit of Democratic Capitalism.* New York: Madison Books, 2000.

Yergin, D. and Stanislaw, J. *The Commanding Heights: The Battle for the World Economy.* New York: Simon and Schuster, 2002.

11. "The Global Mind"

by John R. Cannon, Ph.D.
Alvin A. Cook, Ph.D.
John T. Kelly, D.Sc.
Susan Kelly, B.A.
Hernan Oyarzabal, B.A.

"The Global Mind"

MEANING

Globalization is the preferred choice of free people. Developmentally, free people create global relationships.

Free people do not want to be limited in the contacts they make. They actively seek out people who are different from themselves. Free people search for new ideas and new opportunities to relate with—economically and socially. Most of all, free people are looking for *"Processing Partners"* to help them solve problems and create new opportunities.

This chapter presents the free "global mind". Specifically, it introduces *The New 3Rs of Freedom-Building*: relating, representing, and reasoning. These are processing skills that enable freedom.

The leaders were dubious, even confrontative, regarding a definition of globalization, let alone leadership:

> - *"We don't need another American version of world civilization!"*
>
> - *"Every nation has its own way of doing things!"*
>
> - *"Every culture has its own set of values!"*

Robert R. Carkhuff, consultant on globalization and leadership, personalized his responses in interacting with the leaders:

> - *"You're frustrated by America's assertive leadership!"*
>
> - *"You're disappointed in yourselves that you have not been able to assert your own leadership."*
>
> - *"In some ways, you can identify with our enemies in reacting to the rapid movement toward an integrated global society. As globalization moves further and further ahead, you fall farther and farther behind."*

Carkhuff offered the leaders a choice between two approaches: either a training module in leadership or sharing experiences of the possible. The leaders chose the latter. Carkhuff responded:

> *"So you will not get didactic training. But you will receive the other ingredients of learning — experiential, modeling, and reinforcement. You will learn to process with **'The Global Mind.'**"*

The Learning Experience

Carkhuff began by sharing images of *The Possibilities Community, The Possibilities Culture,* and *The Possibilities Nation.* The leaders responded:

> *"This is perhaps possible. But it is not probable."*

To which Carkhuff responded in kind:

> *"It is both!"*

In interrelating, Carkhuff treated the leaders as another culture. He knew that if they were to help other cultures, they themselves had to be addressed as a culture. Accordingly, Carkhuff processed with the leaders to discriminate their own levels of cultural capital development, or **CCD'**. Altogether their processing work focused on:

- Levels of cultural capital development **(CCD')**,
- Levels of economic capital development **(ECD)**,
- Levels of governance capital development **(GCD)**,
- Levels of community capital development **(CCD)**,
- Levels of organizational capital development **(OCD)**.

The discrimination of these levels of **CCD'** determined the leaders' helpfulness in developing other cultures.

In interacting with the group, Carkhuff employed the human processing paradigm shown in Figure 11-1. As we may note, the paradigm emphasizes the following processing systems:

- **R¹ Relating**
  - Getting images
  - Giving images
  - Merging images

- **R^2 Representing**
    - S^1 Sentences
    - S^2 Systems
    - S^3 Schematics

- **R^3 Reasoning**
    - Expanding alternatives
    - Narrowing to preferred alternative
    - Doing by performing tasks to achieve objectives

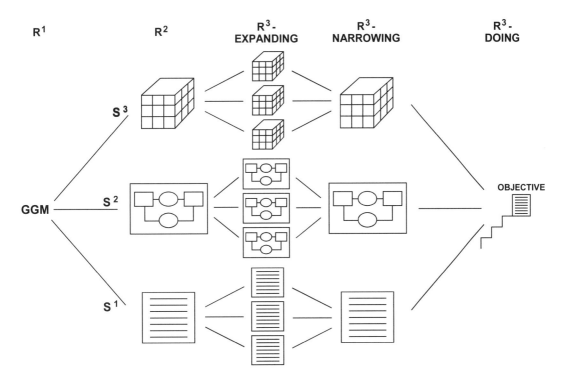

Figure 11-1. The Human Processing Paradigm

These are *The New 3Rs* of processing. They empower participants to process collaboratively and generatively with the great issues of their time.

Relating to Images

In relating, Carkhuff utilized interpersonal processing skills to elicit and develop participants' images of relevant cultural information:

- **Getting** their images,
- **Giving** his image,
- **Merging** images.

"Get – Give – Merge." These are the basic skills of processing.

Getting Images

Carkhuff began by relating to the leaders' frames of reference, especially to their assumptions:

> *"You're not at all certain that capitalistic economics make the world go 'round. But you are commissioned by your mission to help the world go 'round:*
>
> - *The economic integration of markets,*
> - *The liberalization of trade policies.*
>
> *You just don't know how to make this happen."*

Giving Images

In turn, Carkhuff shared his image of globalization:

> *"Ideas make the world go 'round. And 'Big Ideas' make the world go around the fastest. Here are some of the 'Big Ideas' that build to Possibilities Globalization:*
>
> - *Collaborative cultural relating,*
> - *Entrepreneurial free enterprise,*
> - *Direct democratic governance,*
> - *Generative community engines."*

Merging Images

Finally, Carkhuff and the leaders processed to negotiate a merged image of the information. Carkhuff began again with a *"Get"* from the leaders:

> *"What is so different about our positions?"*

To which Carkhuff responded with a *"Give"*:

> *"Probabilities! Your position is* The Probabilities Culture *in operation. You dictate behaviors and attenuate globalization."*

> **Leaders:**
> *"And your position?"*

> **Carkhuff:**
> *"Possibilities!* The Possibilities Culture *provides the menu for self-determination and accelerates globalization."*

> **Leaders:**
> *"Can possibilities and probabilities not exist side by side?"*

Carkhuff:

"They do! But possibilities must drive probabilities 'to do the right things'!

"And all cultures must be able to make their own determinations regarding the levels of **CCD′** *to which they aspire and the level of resources they are willing to commit:*

- *Cultural relating, or Cultural Capital Development* **(CCD′)***;*

- *Economic enterprise, or Economic Capital Development* **(ECD)***;*

- *Democratic governance, or Governance Capital Development* **(GCD)***;*

- *Generative communities, or Community Capital Development* **(CCD)***;*

- *Organizational Capital Development, or* **OCD.**

Thus, the resources that they invest will be related to the benefits they will receive."

Representing Images

In representing, Carkhuff worked with the leaders to develop their images. Basing their approach upon preparatory materials, the group proceeded deductively in developing these images:

- **Schematic** images of multidimensional representations,
- **Systems** images of two-dimensional representations,
- **Sentence** images of one-dimensional verbal representations.

The New 3Ss! These are the basic levels of representing images for processing.

Schematic Images of Leadership

They began deductively with three-dimensional representations of the conditions of the global marketplace within which all cultures are nested (see Figure 11-2). Through these schematic images, the leaders discovered that the requirements of the global marketplace are manifested in the functions of globalization:

> - *CCD' requirements,*
> - *ECD requirements,*
> - *GCD requirements,*
> - *CCD requirements,*
> - *OCD requirements.*

The requirements of the global marketplace are the functions of the conditions of globalization.

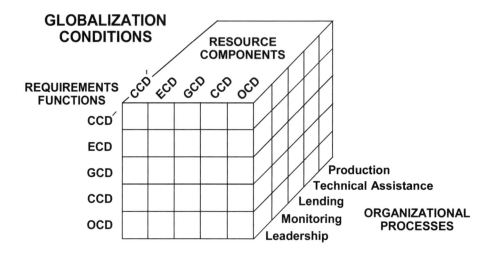

Figure 11-2. Globalization Conditions

In turn, the leaders represented the cultural resources or capacities available for meeting these capital development requirements in their components:

- *CCD' capacities,*
- *ECD capacities,*
- *GCD capacities,*
- *CCD capacities,*
- *OCD capacities.*

The capacities are the resources dedicated to the achievement of globalization requirements.

Finally, the leaders represented the organizational processes by which the resource components were enabled to discharge the requirements functions:

- **Leadership,** *or guidance;*
- **Monitoring,** *or relating;*
- **Lending,** *or resourcing;*
- **Technical Assistance;**
- **Production,** *or delivery.*

To sum, the organizational processes enabled the resource components to accomplish the globalization requirements. These are the conditions within which the leadership model was nested and from which it was derived.

In order to help the leaders understand the leadership model, Carkhuff rotated the globalization conditions deductively, or counter-clockwise (see Figure 11-3). As may be noted, the resource components, or capacities, became the leadership functions: policy, executive, management, supervision, and delivery. In turn, the organizational processes became the components: leadership, monitoring, lending, technical assistance, and production.

Next, the enabling organizational processes were introduced:

- **Goaling** – *Values and requirements,*
- **Inputting** – *Resource inputs,*
- **Processing** – *Transforming processes,*
- **Planning** – *Systematic operations,*
- **Outputting** – *Results outputs.*

Armed with these dimensions, the leaders were now able to define leadership:

"Leadership functions are discharged by organizational components enabled by organizational processes."

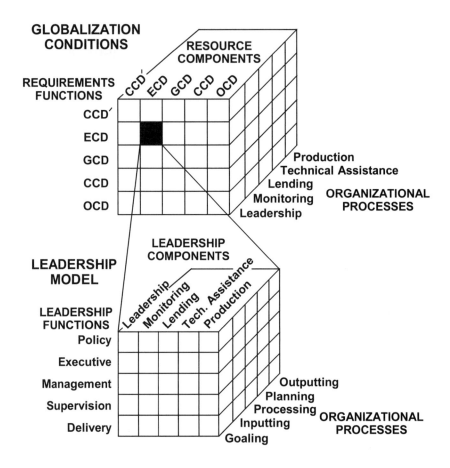

Figure 11-3. The Leadership Model

The leaders derived the leadership standards in the same manner by rotating the leadership model deductively (see Figure 11-4). As may be viewed, the organizational components were rotated to become standards' functions: leadership, monitoring, lending, technical assistance, and production. In turn, the organizational processes were rotated to become standards' components: goaling, inputting, processing, planning, and outputting. Finally, the enabling processes were negotiated as performance standards, as illustrated below (they are presented deductively in Figure 11-4):

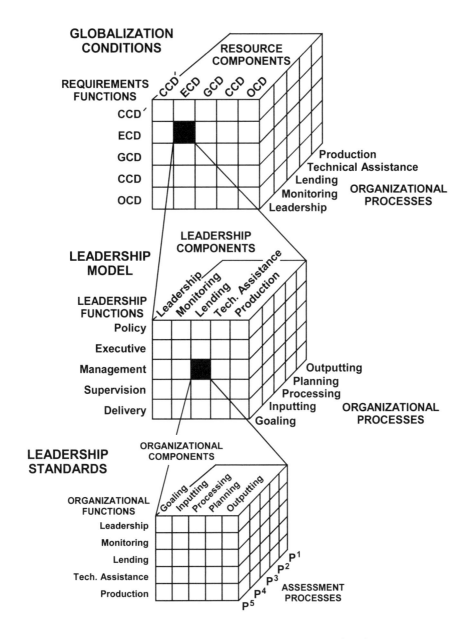

Figure 11-4. The Leadership Standards

- **P^1** — *Performance Criteria,*
- **P^2** — *Production Criteria,*
- **P^3** — *Productivity Criteria,*
- **P^4** — *Profit Criteria,*
- **P^5** — *Profit Growth.*

Together, the leaders defined the standards for leadership:

> *"Organizational functions are discharged by organizational processing components evaluated by organizational performance standards."*

Systems Images of Leadership

A closer view of the leadership models yields the particulars of the functions, components, and processes derived from globalization conditions (see Figure 11-5). The leaders emphasized balanced-world-trade functions. All other functions are nested in this as follows:

- **Policy** — *Balanced world trade,*
- **Executive** — *Sustainable growth architecture,*
- **Management** — *Stable exchange rates,*
- **Supervision** — *Orderly monetary devaluations,*
- **Delivery** — *Orderly monetary corrections.*

These are the driving functions of their leadership model.

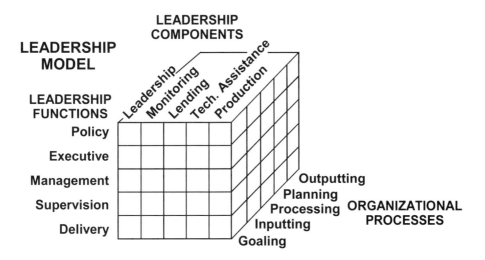

Figure 11-5. Specifics of Leadership Model

Carkhuff then worked with the leaders to define the operations of the leadership systems derived from the leadership models and globalization conditions (see Figure 11-6).

Results Outputs

The leaders determined that the systems are driven by the results outputs:

> - ***Trade*** — *Balanced world trade,*
> - ***Growth*** — *Sustainable growth architecture,*
> - ***Exchange*** — *Stable exchange rates,*
> - ***Devaluations*** — *Orderly monetary devaluations,*
> - ***Corrections*** — *Orderly monetary corrections.*

These are the results outputs that drive their leadership system.

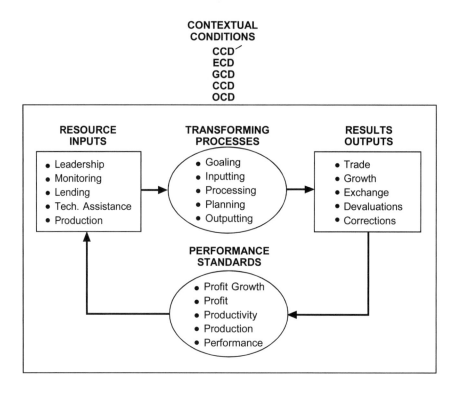

Figure 11-6. Leadership System

Resource Inputs

In turn, the leaders discerned that the resource inputs that are invested to achieve these results outputs are nested in leadership:

- *Leadership,*
- *Monitoring,*
- *Lending,*
- *Technical Assistance,*
- *Production.*

Again, these organizational components are dedicated to achieving the leadership functions derived from globalization.

Transforming Processes

Again, the leaders recalled that the organizational processes are the transforming processes that convert the organizational resource inputs into organizational leadership results outputs:

- *Goaling,*
- *Inputting,*
- *Processing,*
- *Planning,*
- *Outputting.*

Remember that the organizational processes enable the organizational inputs to be transformed into leadership outputs.

Contextual Conditions

The leaders derived conditions under which the transformation of resource inputs into results outputs occurs from our globalization models:

- *CCD', or Cultural Capital Development,*
- *ECD, or Economic Capital Development,*
- *GCD, or Governance Capital Development,*
- *CCD, or Community Capital Development,*
- *OCD, or Organization Capital Development.*

Thus, the transformation of organizational inputs into leadership outputs is modified by the conditions of globalization.

Performance Standards

Finally, the leaders discriminated the levels of leadership results as measured by performance standards or criteria, presented inductively below:

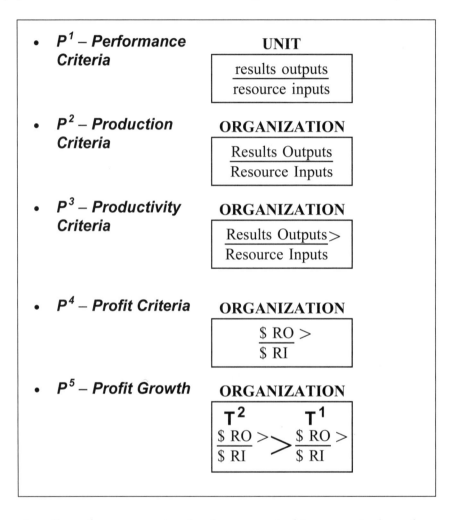

Once again, all performance standards are nested in some index of productivity, profit, or growth as they measure the results outputs of leadership.

To sum, the leaders defined their system operationally:

> *"Leadership-driven inputs are transformed into trade-driven outputs by organizational processes under modifying globalization conditions and with elevated performance standards."*

In short, they could achieve their desired results at the highest levels by processing their resource inputs at the highest levels.

Sentence Images of Leadership

The leaders translated this operational definition directly into a leadership program statement based upon the fundamental interrogatives of *"5W2H"* (see Table 11-1). As may be noted, the leadership mission was stated in simple terms at the lowest level of sentence formation. In short, this means that the leaders could accomplish what they set out to accomplish through modeling systems and their operations.

Table 11-1. The Leadership Mission

BASIC INTERROGATIVES	OPERATIONS
Who?	Leadership-driven components
What?	discharge trade-driven functions
How?	by way of organizational processes
Why?	to balance trade and to "architect" growth
Where and When?	under **CCD'**-driven conditions
How Well?	at high levels of performance standards.

Historically, leaders would set out to produce a sentence-based image of leadership. It would not be derived from relating to images: *Get – Give – Merge.* It would not be represented dimensionally: *Sentences – Systems – Schematics.* It would not enable the leaders to achieve their goals of leadership under the conditions of globalization.

Moreover, this process would not enable the leaders to process with the images of information. Without information representation, there is no reasoning! Without relating, there is no representation!

Reasoning With Images

In reasoning, Carkhuff employed the human processing paradigm to process with the group (again see Figure 11-1):

- **Expanding** images of operations,

- **Narrowing** images of operations,

- **Doing** or performing the steps to implement the preferred images.

Expanding and narrowing are the critical phases of all human processing.

Expanding Images

Utilizing the leadership system, then, the leaders expanded the operations. Here is what they generated.

---

1. **Expanded Results Outputs**
   The driving world-trade functions nested all of the other functions: growth architecture, exchange rates, devaluations, and corrections.

   - **Balanced → Imbalanced World Trade.** With expanding, the leaders recognized that, in many instances, nations were imbalanced in their trading initiatives. Yet they were breaking ground in new and potentially growthful areas. Indeed, often financial investments followed these imbalanced initiatives in the most promising areas of trade.

- **Sustainable → Continuous growth architecture.** With expanding, the leaders acknowledged that growing was not a plan but a process. While they can "architect" the process, they cannot "architect" the plan. Things change!

- **Stable → Continuously changing currency-exchange rates.** The leaders recognized that nothing—no thing—in God's universe is stable, least of all exchange rates. They expanded to continuously changing exchange rates.

- **Orderly → Ongoing currency devaluations.** The leaders recognized that currency devaluations were neither stable nor orderly—but ongoing!

- **Orderly → Ongoing currency corrections.** Ditto for orderly corrections! The leaders likewise expanded to ongoing and continuous corrections in monetary rates.

In short, the original functions had been dedicated to stasis in a world of continuous change. The expansions were dedicated to aligning with the changes and, indeed, stimulating them.

2. **Expanded Resource Inputs**
   The driving leadership inputs nested all of the other expanding resource inputs: monitoring, lending, technical assistance, and production.

   - **Leadership → Inclusive leadership and guidance.** In expanding, the leaders acknowledged that exclusive leadership must be transformed into inclusive leadership that incorporates the needs of changing cultures and nations.

- **Monitoring → Relating to cultural needs.** Again, the leaders recognized that relating to the internal phenomenological experience of the cultures was more powerful than monitoring them exclusively from an external frame of reference.

- **Lending → Resourcing cultural initiatives.** Once again, the leaders recognized the synergistic benefits of processing to align with the success of cultural initiatives rather than simply lending money and monitoring its uses.

- **Technological → Mutual processing assistance.** By expanding their vision of technological assistance to emphasize processing, the leaders acknowledged the empowerment of mutual processing as opposed to the dependency of planning.

- **Production → Mutual production or delivery.** By expanding their vision of producer production to incorporate consumer production, the leaders emphasized mutual production for mutual benefit.

In short, the original components had been dedicated to the discharge of static functions. The expansions were dedicated to relating and aligning with the requirements for changing functions under changing conditions.

3. **Expanded Transforming Processes**
    The greatest expansions took place in the transforming processes where the organizational processes were transformed into **NCD** systems.

    - **Goaling → MCD,** or marketplace positioning;
    - **Inputting → OCD,** or organizational alignment;
    - **Processing → HCD,** or human processing;
    - **Planning → ICD,** or information modeling;
    - **Outputting → mCD,** or mechanical tooling.

In short, the original enabling organizational processes were expanded into empowering **NCD** systems: **MCD, OCD, HCD, ICD, mCD.**

To sum, the functions, components, and processes of the original leadership systems were expanded to change with the changing conditions, changing systems, and changing operations. In short, leadership is continuously reprocessed and redesigned to become a generator and innovator of change.

Narrowing Images

Again, utilizing the leadership system, the leaders were able to narrow the operations according to their original globalization values and requirements.

---

1. **Narrowed Results Outputs**
   - Changing balances in world trade,
   - Continuous growth architecture,
   - Continuous changing exchange rates,
   - Ongoing currency devaluations,
   - Ongoing currency corrections.

In short, the results outputs were narrowed to align with continuous change.

---

2. **Narrowed Resource Inputs**
   - Inclusive leadership and guidance,
   - Responsive relating to cultural needs,
   - Personalized resourcing of cultural initiatives,
   - Mutual processing for technical assistance,
   - Mutual production for delivery.

In short, the resource inputs were narrowed so they could be guided by continuous relating for continuous change.

---

3. **Narrowed Transforming Processes**
   - **MCD,** or continuous marketplace positioning;
   - **OCD,** or continuous organizational alignment;
   - **HCD,** or continuous human processing;
   - **ICD,** or continuous information modeling;
   - **mCD,** or continuous mechanical tooling.

In short, the transforming processes were narrowed to the continuous processing of **NCD** systems: **MCD, OCD, HCD, ICD, mCD.**

Doing or Implementing Images

Working with the human processing paradigm, the leaders then presented the newly narrowed leadership system (see Figure 11-7). Together, they defined the leadership system operationally:

---

*"Relating leadership inputs are transformed by **NCD** processing systems into changing trade outputs."*

In short, if we want to be helpful in changing cultures or nations, then we must relate to their changing needs and process with them at all levels.

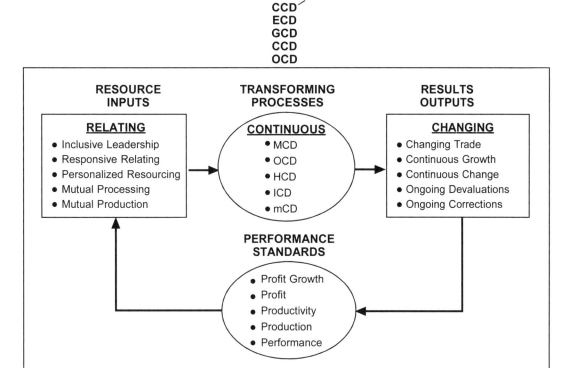

Figure 11-7. Narrowed Leadership System

The actual doing, or acting upon, of the newly developed systems is a function of developing and implementing programs to achieve the objectives presented: resource inputs, transforming processes, and results outputs.

Leadership Implications

The leadership skills were modeled by Carkhuff in processing with the leaders. We may view the skills in a simplified form in *The Leadership Matrix* (see Figure 11-8). As may be viewed, the cultural capital development is the function of leadership: **CCD′, ECD, GCD.** The leadership skills dedicated to accomplishing these functions are *The New 3Rs* of processing: R^1, R^2, R^3. This means that we must process in order to achieve each function of cultural capital development. Carkhuff modeled leadership by relating in this manner to the culture of the leaders. The leaders will demonstrate leadership similarly, by relating to their nations or cultures in this manner.

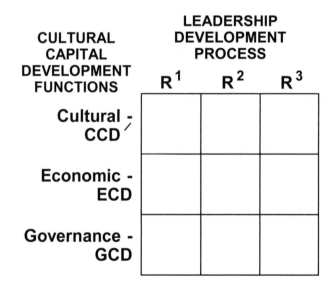

Figure 11-8. The Leadership Matrix

In developing leadership skills, Carkhuff modeled the following:

- **Relating:** Get – Give – Merge;
- **Representing:** Sentences – Systems – Schematics;
- **Reasoning:** Expanding – Narrowing – Doing.

The New 3Rs were addressed at every level of cultural capital development: **CCD', ECD, GCD.**

Indeed, there were testimonials by the leaders:

- *"This is the first time that we have understood leadership systems."*

- *"You have modeled them for us."*

- *"We have experienced them directly."*

To which Carkhuff responded directly:

"It remains for you to be reinforced differentially:

- *Rewarded for skilled performance,*
- *Extinguished for non-performance,*
- *Punished for malpractice."*

The leaders responded in kind:

"This is also the way we must differentially reinforce our client states."

Carkhuff:
"Before attempting to help another culture, you must first help yourselves."

Leaders:
"We cannot relate interdependently if we ourselves do not process interdependently."

> **Carkhuff:**
> *"Continuous interdependent processing is the culminating condition of possibilities!"*

> **Leaders:**
> *"Ultimately, globalization is a function of continuous interdependent processing."*

> **Carkhuff:**
> *"Without continuous interdependent processing, there can be no continuous growth — in organizations, communities, cultures, nations, or global village."*

In this context, *"The Invisible Hand"* of economics has been extended by *"The Global Mind"* to give us a profound understanding of self-interest in the integrated and elevated global society:

- **Cultural relatedness** whereby our neighbor's interests are our interests;

- **Economic enterprise** whereby generative people are empowered to pursue their own purposes;

- **Political democracy** whereby enlightened people vote with trade and reciprocity.

Indeed, this is *"The Global Mind"* of infinite, virtual brainpower that is interdependently the generator of wealth and the will of the people. It is only transitionally the generator of the intentionality of those who lead.

In summary, ultimately, leading is helping. And leading nations toward globalization is the most profound level of helping. It means moving forward while reaching back to help as many people as possible live the highest-quality lives in the highest-quality environments.

References

Carkhuff, R. R. *Globalization and Leadership.* Keynote address and modules: International Monetary Fund, Wye Woods Conference Center, Queenstown, MD. December 8, 2001.

Carkhuff, R. R. and Berenson, B. G. *The Possibilities Leader.* Amherst, MA: HRD Press, 2000.

Carkhuff, R. R. and Berenson, B. G. *The Possibilities Organization.* Amherst, MA: HRD Press, 2000.

Carkhuff, R. R. and Berenson, B. G. *The Possibilities Economics.* Amherst, MA: HRD Press, 2002.

Carkhuff, R. R. and Berenson, B. G. *Possibilities Thinking.* Amherst, MA: HRD Press, 2002.

Carkhuff, R. R., Berenson, B. G. and Griffin, A. H. *The Possibilities Culture.* Amherst, MA: HRD Press, 2002.

Carkhuff, R. R., Griffin, A. H. and Berenson, B. G. *The Possibilities Community.* Amherst, MA: HRD Press, 2002.

Irwin, D. A. *Free Trade Under Fire.* Princeton, NJ: Princeton University Press, 2002.

IV. Summary and Transition

12. The Possibilities Leader

by Robert R. Carkhuff, Ph.D.
Bernard G. Berenson, Ph.D.
Andrew H. Griffin, D.Ed.
John T. Kelly, D.Sc.
Rob Owen, M.B.A.

The Possibilities Leader

MEANING

Possibilities Leaders are *Freedom-Builders*. Developmentally, free nations and free people take leadership and responsibility for freedom-building.

Freedom-building begins with a vision of freedom for: individuals, communities, nations, and cultures. Guided by *The Freedom-Building Model*, possibilities leaders go about freedom-building activities: positioning, reinforcing, and empowering.

In this chapter we learn about the *Freedom-Building* activities of: positioning and communicating a "high-ground" for freedom in cultural relating, economic enterprise and governmental support; reinforcing differentially; and empowering people with freedom-building skills.

The 20th century has been termed by many as *"The American Century."* Indeed, America has been the model for collaborative cultural relating, capitalistic wealth generation, and representative democratic governance. In so being, American modeled the powerful *Freedom-Building* ingredients of the 20th century:

- **Collaborative relating,**
- **Capitalistic economics,**
- **Democratic governance.**

These *Freedom-Building* ingredients provide the foundation for *Freedom-Building* in the 21st century.

Near the end of the 20th century, America moved again to assert leadership in the 21st century:

> *Sometime in the last decade of the twentieth century, [American] civilization crossed a momentous threshold. It moved from shaping cultures based upon past traditions to generating cultures to meet future requirements. Because of spiraling changes in technology-driven economies, the historic traditions no longer suffice. Scientific and technological* 'breakthroughs' *have generated robust, new socioeconomic requirements that must be met in order to participate in the marketplace. Our traditional responses, no matter how enduring, are rendered impotent. The requirements that define our new century's culture are prepotent.* (Carkhuff and Berenson, 2000, *Possibilities Organization,* p. xix)

Now in the 21st century, the standards for an integrated and elevated global society are already defined:

- **Interdependent cultural relating,**
- **Free market economies,**
- **Free democratic governance.**

Let us summarize these dimensions in the form of *The Globalization Principle:*

> *Interdependent cultural relations are accomplished by free market economics enabled by free democratic governance.*

By interdependent cultural relating, we do not simply mean collaborative exchanges between cultures. We mean *"mutual processing for mutual benefit."*

By free market economics, we do not simply mean capitalism as it has been practiced historically. We mean entrepreneurially-driven free enterprise enabled by new capital ingredients that now account for 85% of the variability in economic productivity growth: marketplace, organization, human, information, and mechanical capital.

By free democratic governance, we do not simply mean representative governance as it has been practiced historically. We mean the direct democracy within which *"enlightened citizens"* can participate, contribute, and lead.

It is within America's grasp to lead us into *"The Global Century"* by becoming both model and agent for change toward:

- **Interdependent cultural relating,**
- **Free enterprise economics,**
- **Free democratic governance.**

These are the still-evolving requirements for participation in *The Global Village* and its marketplace.

Freedom-Building Functions

The first decision that a nation such as the United States must make is whether it is going to lead, follow, or fiddle in relation to developing an integrated global society. We may represent the choices as different levels of functions on a leadership scale (see Table 12-1). As we may note, the scale ranges from leading and contributing to observing and detracting or destroying.

Table 12-1.
The Leadership Functions

5	Leading
4	Contributing
3	Participating
2	Observing
1	Detracting

For example, decisions have been made to accomplish the following leadership functions:

- Assuming *"Commanding Heights Positioning,"*
- Generating *"Differential Reinforcement Policies,"*
- Implementing *"Human Empowerment Programs."*

In choosing these functions, a nation such as America dedicates itself to providing leadership in moving toward the global society. They are the **Freedom-Building Functions.** They depend upon the **Freedom-Building Components** for their accomplishment.

Freedom-Building Components

The next series of decisions that a culture or a nation must make emphasizes the **Freedom-Building Components** required to discharge the desired leadership functions. The critical components involve the following: cultural relating, economic enterprise, and governance support.

Cultural Relating

The second decision that a culture or nation must make, then, is the level at which it will relate to other nations in discharging, or accomplishing, the desired leadership functions. We may represent the first of these **Freedom-Building Components, "Cultural Relating,"** with a relating scale (see Table 12-2). As we may note, the scale ranges from interdependent and collaborative to dependent and reactive.

Table 12-2. Cultural Relating

5	**Interdependent**
4	**Collaborative**
3	**Independent**
2	**Competitive**
1	**Dependent**

For example, as part of its differential reinforcement policy, the American leadership may select to function at a collaborative level with *"Growing Nations,"* at an independent but vigilant level with *"Undecided Nations,"* and at a competitive level with *"Detracting Nations."* While its intentions are dedicated to be interdependent with *"Growers,"* it is not yet prepared for *"mutual processing for mutual benefits."*

Economic Enterprise

The third decision that a culture or nation must make is the level of economic enterprise that it will dedicate to its desired level of cultural relating. We may represent the second of these **Freedom-Building Components,** *"Economic Enterprise,"* with an enterprise scale (see Table 12-3). As we may note, the scale ranges from free and capitalistic enterprise to command and control economies.

Table 12-3. Economic Enterprise

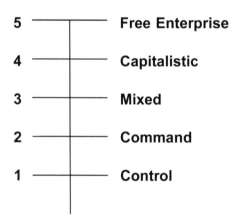

For example, the American leadership may select the capitalistic level of enterprise to accomplish its desired level of collaborative relating. While its intentions are dedicated to free enterprise, it may not yet be prepared for the **Entrepreneurial-Driven, Free Enterprise Economics** that will be accessible by empowerment to the other nations of the world.

Governance Support

The fourth decision that a nation must make is the level of governance support to be dedicated to enabling the desired level of economic enterprise. We may represent the third of these **Freedom-Building Components, "***Governance Support,***"** with a governance scale (see Table 12-4). As we may note, the levels range from free, democratic, and representative governance to authoritarian and totalitarian governance.

Table 12-4. Governance Support

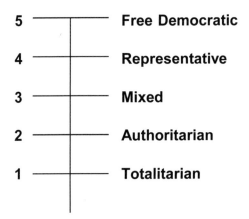

5	**Free Democratic**
4	**Representative**
3	**Mixed**
2	**Authoritarian**
1	**Totalitarian**

For example, the American leadership may select the representative level of democratic governance to enable its capitalistic enterprise to accomplish its desired level of cultural relating. While its intentions are dedicated to free and direct democratic governance, and it has the electronic means available to it, it has not yet prepared the *"enlightened citizenry"* that direct democratic governance requires.

Freedom-Building Process

The next series of decisions revolve around the **Freedom-Building Processes** that a nation must implement in order to enable or empower the **Freedom-Building Components** to accomplish their desired leadership functions. The critical processes emphasize the *New Capital Development,* or *NCD,* technologies that enable **Freedom-Building Functions** (Table 12-5):

- *Marketplace Capital Development,* or *MCD,* technologies that position communities or organizations in the marketplace;

- *Organizational Capital Development,* or *OCD,* technologies that align organization resources to implement marketplace positioning;

- *Human Capital Development,* or *HCD,* technologies that empower people to process to implement organizational resource alignment;

- *Information Capital Development,* or *ICD,* technologies that model information to implement human processing;

- *Mechanical Capital Development,* or *mCD,* technologies that produce mechanical tools to implement information modeling.

Together, the **NCD** technologies comprise the processes that enable the components to achieve the **Freedom-Building Functions.**

Table 12-5. New Capital Development Technologies

5 ————— **MCD - Marketplace Capital Development**

4 ————— **OCD - Organization Capital Development**

3 ————— **HCD - Human Capital Development**

2 ————— **ICD - Information Capital Development**

1 ————— **mCD - Mechanical Capital Development**

Freedom-Building Model

The functions, components, and processes may be brought together in *The Freedom-Building Model* (see Figure 12-1). As may be viewed, the **Freedom-Building Functions** emphasize leadership:

- *"Commanding Heights" Positioning,*
- *"Differential Reinforcement" Policies,*
- *"Human Empowerment" Programs.*

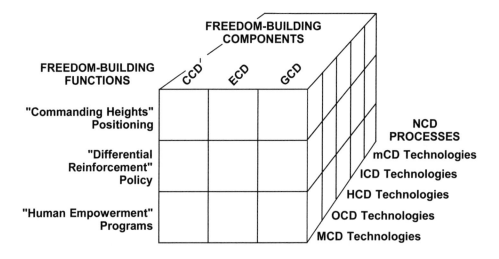

Figure 12-1. The Freedom-Building Model

In turn, the **Freedom-Building Components** emphasize and include *Cultural Capital Development:*

- **CCD'**, or **Cultural Capital Development;**
- **ECD**, or **Economic Capital Development;**
- **GCD**, or **Governance Capital Development.**

Finally, the **Freedom-Building Processes** emphasize **NCD** technologies:

- **MCD Technologies,**
- **OCD Technologies,**
- **HCD Technologies,**
- **ICD Technologies,**
- **mCD Technologies.**

As may be noted, potentially every level of processes interacts with every level of components and functions, and vice versa: components with functions and processes; functions with components and processes. For example, this means that **HCD Technologies** such as *"Get – Give – Merge"* have significant impact upon all components **(CCD', ECD, GCD)** and, thus, all functions **(Positioning, Policy, Programs).** Again, all levels of all dimensions potentially impact all levels of all other dimensions.

Together, these dimensions define *The Freedom-Building Model:*

> *Leadership-driven positioning, policies, and programs achieved by cultural relating, economic enterprise, and governance support enabled by* **NCD** *technologies.*

In short, in *Freedom-Building,* as in life, we lead by how we relate, initiate, and support our leadership functions.

The current U.S. model falls far short of *The Freedom-Building Model* (see Figure 12-2). In terms of **Freedom-Building Functions,** we focus on administering only limited policy, the punishment of enemies.

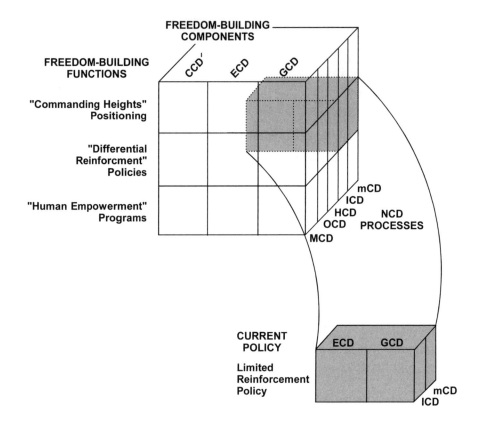

Figure 12-2. Current Freedom-Building Model

In this context, we address only limited versions of **Freedom-Building Components**, represented in our terms by the march of international capitalism **(ECD)** and representative democracy **(GCD).** In addition, we emphasize only mechanical **(mCD)** and information capital development **(ICD)** in our **Infrastructure Building** to enable economic and governance development.

Without *"Commanding Heights"* positioning, then, we may not administer *"Differential Reinforcement"* policy:

- **Positively reinforcing those countries who are moving toward growth;**

- **Observing diligently those countries who have not committed to growth;**

- **Punishing those countries that are committed to the destruction of others.**

In other words, we must first become *"potent reinforcers"* by modeling the dimensions before we can become *"differential reinforcers"* as agents of change.

Moreover, we cannot have an enduring influence upon others unless we conduct *"Human Empowerment"* programs: programs that relate, empower, and free the target populations to acquire, apply, and transfer the growth conditions to their own purposes and values.

The Freedom-Building Model may be viewed in sharp relief in *The Freedom-Building System* (see Figure 12-3). Here **CCD'**-driven resource inputs are transformed into commanding-driven results outputs by **NCD** technological processes; these transforming processes occur under global conditions emphasizing relating, empowering, and freeing; these transforming processes are measured by performance standards emphasizing movement toward possibilities cultures, nations, and globalization.

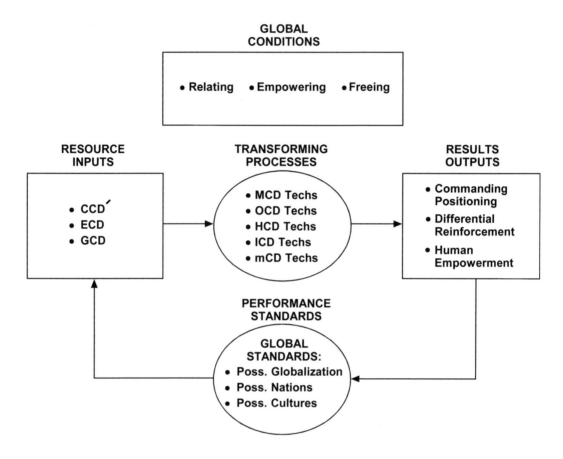

GLOBAL CONDITIONS
- Relating
- Empowering
- Freeing

RESOURCE INPUTS
- CCD´
- ECD
- GCD

TRANSFORMING PROCESSES
- MCD Techs
- OCD Techs
- HCD Techs
- ICD Techs
- mCD Techs

RESULTS OUTPUTS
- Commanding Positioning
- Differential Reinforcement
- Human Empowerment

PERFORMANCE STANDARDS

GLOBAL STANDARDS:
- Poss. Globalization
- Poss. Nations
- Poss. Cultures

Figure 12-3. The Freedom-Building System

In turn, *The Freedom-Building Mission* may be summarized verbally:

COMPONENTS	*Freedom-Building Components*
FUNCTIONS	*are transformed into Freedom-Building Functions*
PROCESSES	*by NCD Processes*
CONDITIONS	*under Global Conditions*
STANDARDS	*at measurable levels of movement toward Globalization Standards.*

We may also express this as shown in Table 12-6.

Table 12-6. The Freedom-Building Mission

Freedom-Building Components …

- **CCD′**
- **ECD**
- **GCD**

are transformed into **Freedom-Building Functions …**

- **Commanding Positioning**
- **Differential Reinforcement Policy**
- **Human Empowerment Programs**

by **Freedom-Building Processes …**

- **MCD Technologies**
- **OCD Technologies**
- **HCD Technologies**
- **ICD Technologies**
- **mCD Technologies**

under **Global Conditions …**

- **Freeing**
- **Empowering**
- **Relating**

at measurable levels of movement toward **Globalization Standards …**

- **Possibilities Globalization**
- **Possibilities Nations**
- **Possibilities Cultures**

For America, this means that we can become prepotent reinforcers by assuming *"Commanding Heights Positioning."* It means that we can administer *"Differential Reinforcement Policies"* with those nations moving toward, away from, or against globalization. It means that we can implement *"Human Empowerment Programs"* that enable people to work interdependently and synergistically to generate a newly integrated and elevated global society.

In transition, leadership in *Freedom-Building* means that America is truly *"The Great Experiment"* for *The Global Vision,* just as it was 250 years earlier for leadership in an evolving freedom, democracy, enterprise, and community:

- **Leadership!**
- **Interdependency!**
- **Free Enterprise!**
- **Free Democracy!**
- **Generative Community!**

References

Carkhuff, R. R. *Globalization and Leadership.* Keynote address and modules: International Monetary Fund, Wye Woods Conference Center, Queenstown, MD. December 8, 2001.

Carkhuff, R. R. and Berenson, B. G. *The New Science of Possibilities. Volume I. The Processing Science.* Amherst, MA: HRD Press, 2000.

Carkhuff, R. R. and Berenson, B. G. *The New Science of Possibilities. Volume II. The Processing Technologies.* Amherst, MA: HRD Press, 2000.

Carkhuff, R. R. and Berenson, B. G. *The Possibilities Leader.* Amherst, MA: HRD Press, 2000.

Carkhuff, R. R. and Berenson, B. G. *The Possibilities Organization.* Amherst, MA: HRD Press, 2000.

Carkhuff, R. R. and Berenson, B. G. *The Possibilities Economics.* Amherst, MA: HRD Press, 2002.

Carkhuff, R. R. and Berenson, B. G. *Possibilities Thinking.* Amherst, MA: HRD Press, 2002.

Carkhuff, R. R., Berenson, B. G., and Griffin, A. H. *The Possibilities Culture.* Amherst, MA: HRD Press, 2002.

Carkhuff, R. R., Griffin, A. H., and Berenson, B. G. *The Possibilities Community.* Amherst, MA: HRD Press, 2002.

Irwin, D. A. *Free Trade Under Fire.* Princeton, NJ: Princeton University Press, 2002.

Novak, M. *The Spirit of Democratic Capitalism.* New York: Madison Books, 2000.

Yergin, D. and Stanislaw, J. *The Commanding Heights: The Battle for the World Economy.* New York: Simon and Schuster, 2002.

13. The Freedom Doctrine— The Architecture for Global Freedom

by Robert R. Carkhuff, Ph.D.
Bernard G. Berenson, Ph.D.
Leonard D. Goodstein, Ph.D.
Andrew H. Griffin, D.Ed.
John T. Kelly, D.Sc.
Rob Owen, M.B.A.

The Freedom Doctrine—
The Architecture for Global Freedom
MEANING

The Freedom Doctrine culminates in a proposal of specific action steps for freedom-building. Proposal details include: *The Freedom Plan*, *The Freedom Center*, *The Freedom Satellites*, and *Freedom Projects*.

This chapter presents a *Freedom-Building* design including: *The Freedom Architecture*, *The Freedom Curriculum*, and *The New Capital Development Curriculum*. Of necessity, all *Freedom-Building* is modified by continuous interdependent processing of constantly changing requirements and continuously evolving values.

The Freedom Doctrine

Freedom-Building is driven by and culminates in **The Freedom Doctrine.** Inherited from its intellectual ancestors, **The Freedom Doctrine** is interwoven in **The American Experience:**

- **The Freedom Doctrine** *assumes that all peoples seek social, economic, and political freedom.*

- **The Freedom Doctrine** *relates freely and empathically to all peoples of all cultures dedicated to these freedoms.*

- **The Freedom Doctrine** *relates freely and reciprocally to all peoples dedicated to becoming free trading partners.*

- **The Freedom Doctrine** *relates freely and democratically to all governments that relate democratically to their citizens.*

- **The Freedom Doctrine** *empowers communities to generate all forms of new capital to enable social, economic, and political freedom.*

In short, **The Freedom Doctrine** matures in the hearts and minds of American citizens. It is offered freely and openly in the best and boldest visions of its leaders for an integrated and elevated global society (see Table 13-1).

Table 13-1. The Freedom Doctrine

I.   To lead freely by relating, empowering, and freeing all peoples dedicated to participating in our integrated and elevated global society;

II.   To relate freely and interdependently with all cultures dedicated to growing in our global society;

III.   To trade freely and reciprocally in a free enterprise marketplace dedicated to mutual growth in our global society;

IV.   To govern freely and democratically within, between, and among all nations in our global society;

V.   To empower our communities freely to generate all forms of new capital in order to produce a spiraling array of products, services, and solutions that benefit all humankind.

The Freedom Processes

The Mission of **The Freedom Doctrine** is defined as follows:

> *The systematic movement of nations toward an integrated and elevated global society.*

In this context, we may view the dimensions of **The Freedom Doctrine** in sharpest relief as follows:

- **Cultural Relating,**
- **Economic Enterprise,**
- **Governance Support.**

These dimensions are central to **Global Freedom** in the 21st century.

At the highest levels of these dimensions, we may define **Global Freedom** in terms of movement toward an integrated and elevated global society (see Table 13-2):

- **Collaborative and interdependent cultural relating,**
- **New capitalistic and free enterprise economics,**
- **Representative and direct democratic governance.**

These **Global Freedom** dimensions, empowered by **Community Capital Development** as the generating engine, will enable any target nation to move systematically toward a place in an integrated and elevated global society.

Table 13-2. Global Freedom Requirements

Levels of Functioning	Cultural Relating—CCD'	Economic Enterprise—ECD	Governance Support—GCD
Leader	Interdependent	Free Enterprise	Free and Direct
Contributor	Collaborative	Capitalistic	Representative
Participant	Independent	Mixed	Mixed
Observer	Competitive	Command	Authoritarian
Detractor	Dependent	Control	Totalitarian

The Freedom Plan

In Figure 13-1, we may view the details of the **Freedom Processes:**

1. The representatives of the target nations are engaged in interactive learning with **The Freedom Center,** the empowering source of skills learning.

2. The representatives develop personal projects with coaching and support from **The Freedom Satellites.**

3. **The Freedom Satellites** draw upon **The Freedom Center** resources to provide national contracts for **Freedom-Building** by the representatives and their nations.

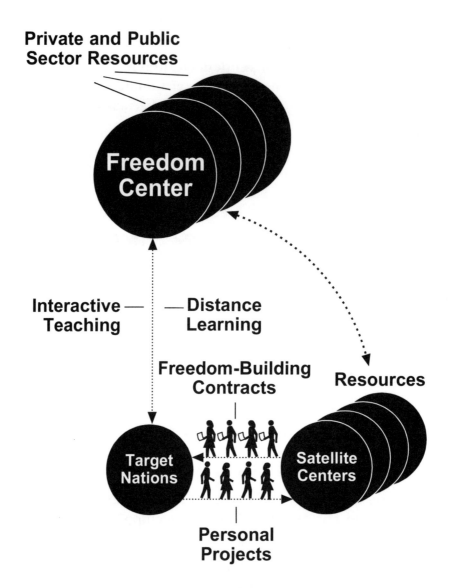

Figure 13-1. The Freedom Center Processes

In Figure 13-2, we may view **The Global Freedom Design.**
The Freedom Functions follow:

- **CCD′** — **Cultural Capital Development,**
- **ECD** — **Economic Capital Development,**
- **GCD** — **Governance Capital Development.**

Together, these dimensions define the functions of the mission of **Global Freedom.**

Similarly, the **Freedom Components** are the **New Capital Development** systems:

- **MCD** — **Marketplace Capital Development,** or marketplace positioning;

- **OCD** — **Organization Capital Development,** or organizational alignment;

- **HCD** — **Human Capital Development,** or human processing;

- **ICD** — **Information Capital Development,** or information modeling;

- **mCD** — **Mechanical Capital Development,** or mechanical tooling.

When these **New Capital Development Components** are systematically related, they define the ingredients that achieve **The Freedom Functions.**

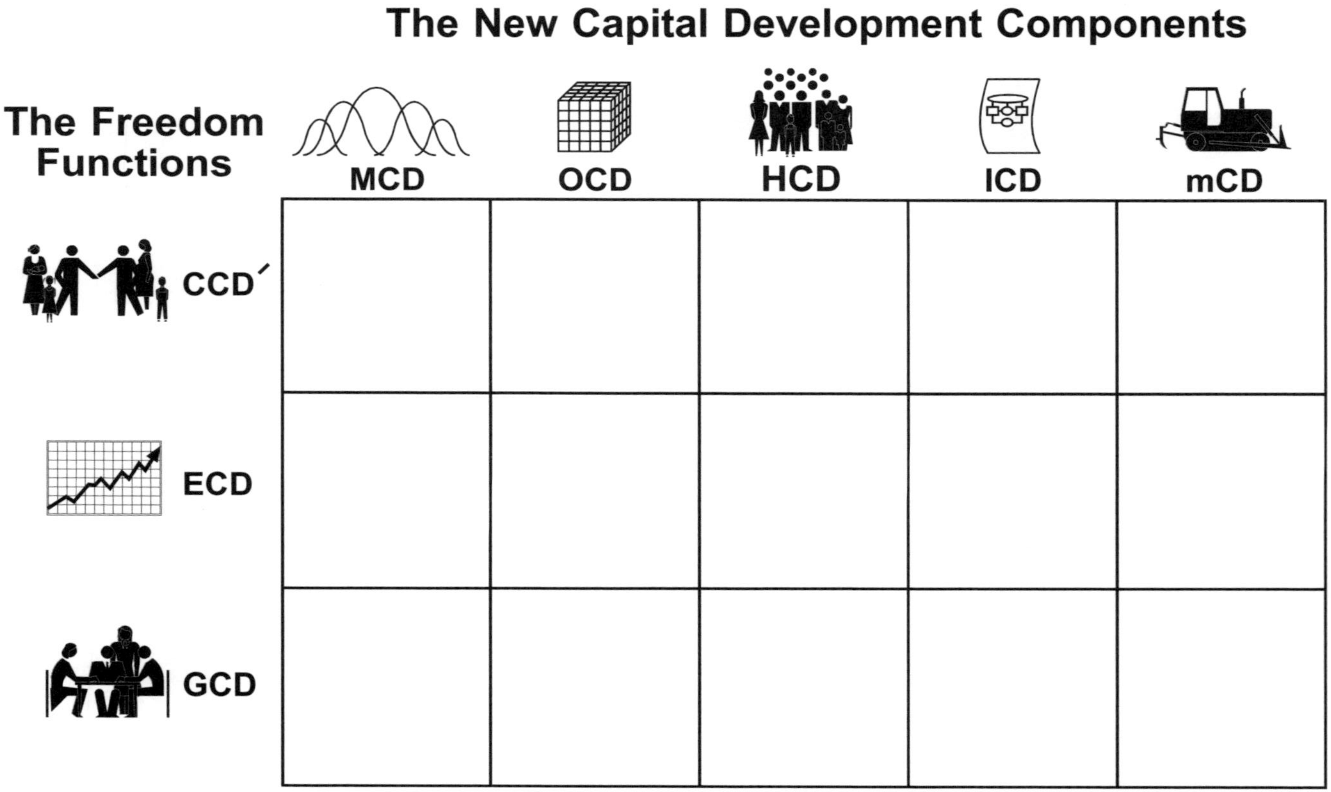

The New Capital Development Components

	MCD	OCD	HCD	ICD	mCD
CCD´					
ECD					
GCD					

The Freedom Functions

Figure 13-2. The Global Freedom Design

In Figure 13-3, we may view the two dimensions of **The Freedom-Building Curriculum:**

- **The Freedom Curriculum,**
- **The New Capital Development Curriculum.**

The Freedom Curriculum is composed of achieving scaled levels of **The Freedom Functions:**

- **Cultural Relating,**
- **Economic Enterprise,**
- **Governance Support.**

In turn, **The New Capital Development Curriculum** is composed of achieving scaled levels of **The NCD Components:**

- **MCD — Marketplace Capital Development,**
- **OCD — Organizational Capital Development,**
- **HCD — Human Capital Development,**
- **ICD — Information Capital Development,**
- **mCD — Mechanical Capital Development.**

Again, **The NCD Components** empower us to achieve **The Freedom Functions.**

These components and functions define **The Freedom Design and Curricula.** Together, this design and curricula define *The Freedom Doctrine for Global Freedom in the 21st Century Integrated and Elevated Global Society.*

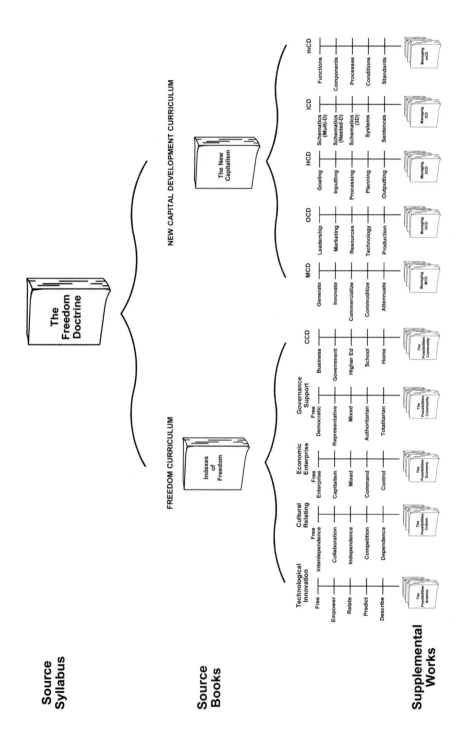

Figure 13-3. The Freedom-Building Curriculum

The Freedom Architecture

We may view **The Freedom Architecture** of **The Freedom Doctrine** in Table 13-3. As may be noted, growthful nations move developmentally through the following levels or stages:

- **From detractive and destructive,**
- **Through observing and participating,**
- **To contributing and leading.**

These developmental stages hold for all of **The Freedom Functions:**

- **Cultural relating from dependency to interdependency,**
- **Economic enterprise from control to free enterprise,**
- **Governance support from totalitarian to free democratic.**

Table 13-3. The Freedom Architecture

THE FREEDOM FUNCTIONS

Stages of Freedom-Building	Cultural Relating	Economic Enterprise	Governance Support	Stages of Civilization
Leader	Free Interdependent	Free Enterprise	Free Democratic	21st Century
Contributor	Collaborative	Capitalistic	Representative	Late 20th Century
Participant	Independent	Mixed	Mixed	Mid 20th Century
Observer	Competitive	Command	Authoritarian	Early 20th Century
Detractor	Dependent	Control	Totalitarian	Pre-20th Century

GROWTH ↑

SURVIVAL

Together, the *Freedom-Building* stages of **The Freedom Functions** define **The Freedom Architecture** for the movement of nations toward membership in the global village and its marketplace:

- **From Pre-20th Century nations,**
- **Through Early, Middle and Late 20th Century nations,**
- **To 21st Century nations.**

In the context of **The Freedom Doctrine,** the implementation of **The Freedom Architecture** would accomplish the following functions:

- **Total immersion in free and interdependent cultural relations through interactive learning and cross-cultural fertilization;**

- **Total immersion in free and democratic governance through personalized project development;**

- **Total immersion in free enterprise economics through outsourcing to private-sector enterprises to implement local, regional, and national projects.**

In so doing, the implementation of **The Freedom Architecture** would emphasize the following principles:

- **Targeting the future policymakers for empowerment;**

- **Targeting the current leaders for awareness;**

- **Making the process voluntary and self-determined in all phases.**

The Freedom Architecture confers the following benefits:

- **Growth architecture before survival infrastructure;**

- **Exemplary social, economic, and political leadership in movement toward embracing freedom;**

- **A continuous interdependent processing model for other troubled nations to follow.**

In summary, **The Freedom Doctrine** emphasizes the commitment of leadership to an integrated and elevated global society empowered by the **New Capital** generated by the community:

- **Leading by freeing all peoples,**
- **Relating by collaborating freely,**
- **Economics by free enterprise,**
- **Governance by free democracy,**
- **Empowerment by free community.**

Just as our founders realized **The Freedom Doctrine** of their intellectual ancestors, so will we actualize and memorialize our contributions of freedom to future generations.

In transition, **The Freedom Architecture** demonstrates one huge step toward the development of **The Freedom Doctrine:**

Rolling Freedom Forward!

References

Berenson, B. G. and Carkhuff, R. R. *The Possibilities Mind.* Amherst, MA: HRD Press, 2001.

Carkhuff, R. R. and Berenson, B. G. *The New Science of Possibilities. Volumes I and II.* Amherst, MA: HRD Press, 2000.

Carkhuff, R. R. and Berenson, B. G. *The Possibilities Leader.* Amherst, MA: HRD Press, 2000.

Carkhuff, R. R. and Berenson, B. G. *The Possibilities Organization.* Amherst, MA: HRD Press, 2000.

Carkhuff, R. R. and Berenson, B. G. *Possibilities Thinking.* Amherst, MA: HRD Press, 2002.

Carkhuff, R. R. and Berenson, B. G. *The Possibilities Economics.* Amherst, MA: HRD Press, 2002.

Carkhuff, R. R., Berenson, B. G. and Griffin, A. H. *The Possibilities Culture.* Amherst, MA: HRD Press, 2002.

Carkhuff, R. R., Carkhuff, C. J., and Cohen, B. *IP⁵D – Integrated Process Development: The Possibilities Business in the Possibilities Economy.* Amherst, MA: HRD Press, 2002.

Carkhuff, R. R., Carkhuff, C. J. and Kelly, J. T. *The GICCA Curve: The Possibilities Marketplace.* Amherst, MA: HRD Press, 2002.

Carkhuff, R. R., Griffin, A. H. and Berenson, B. G. *The Possibilities Community.* Amherst, MA: HRD Press, 2002.

Novak, M. *The Spirit of Democratic Capitalism.* New York: Madison Books, 2000.

O'Driscoll, G. P., Feulner, E. J., and O'Grady, M. A. *2003 Index of Economic Freedom.* Washington, DC: Heritage Foundation, 2003.

Yergin, D. and Stanislaw, J. *The Commanding Heights: The Battle for the World Economy.* New York: Simon and Schuster, 2002.

EPILOG
…Or What's Our Brainpower For?
by John T. Kelly, D.Sc.

More than anything else, Carkhuff and Berenson represent change.

In *The Age of the New Capitalism* (1988), they prepared for the entrepreneurially driven, free enterprise market, one that displaced the financial capital ingredients with the new capital ingredients: marketplace, organization, human, information, and mechanical.

In *The New Science of Possibilities* (2000), these scientists generated new possibilistic processing systems to drive our old probabilistic planning systems to achieve new scientific functions:

- *Relating to all phenomenal experience,*
- *Empowering all phenomenal potential,*
- *Freeing all phenomenal potential to seek their own changeable destinies.*

Now in *The Freedom Doctrine — The Architecture for Global Freedom,* they and their associates detail the applications and transfers for *Freedom-Building* in the global village:

- **Interdependently related cultures,**
- **Free enterprise economics,**
- **Free democratic governance.**

Let us not forget the **New Capital Development (NCD)** systems, for they define the **New Capital Development** ingredients and, in so doing, establish capitalism as a theory of change. We see this clearly in the **NCD** systems themselves, which include:

- Communities and corporations that are continuously repositioning themselves in the marketplace — **Marketplace Capital Development;**

- Organizations that are continuously realigning their resources with the marketplace positioning — **Organizational Capital Development;**

- People who are continuously generating new and better ideas for products, services, and solutions — **Human Capital Development;**

- Data that are continuously transformed into *"real information"* based upon information modeling — **Information Capital Development;**

- Mechanical tools that are continuously modified to meet the requirements of the information models generated by the human processing—**Mechanical Capital Development.**

Building upon the **NCD** foundation, these scientists and their colleagues have demonstrated the power of *Freedom-Building:*

- **CCD′ -** *Cultural Capital Development,*
- **ECD -** *Economic Capital Development,*
- **GCD -** *Governance Capital Development.*

In other words, **The New Capital Development Components** converge upon **The Freedom Functions** in exquisitely engineered organic-processing architecture. To support their conclusions, Carkhuff and Berenson provide an economic database that indicates that *the dimensions of **NCD** account for the preponderance of economic growth.*

In short, Carkhuff and Berenson have defined change in terms of future requirements and values and then have positioned us to maximize meeting both at the highest levels. For Americans, this is a natural evolution, a further advancement for a people who were the *"experiment"* for the world society.

The Declaration of Interdependence

The American Revolution was a War of Independence. It was fought to free the colonies of the pernicious and coercive burdens imposed upon it by the exclusive mentality of the mother country.

The Global Revolution is a War of Interdependence. It is being fought to free world citizenry of the pernicious and coercive burdens of the exclusive mentality of the old probabilistic ways of thinking.

For example, the central theme of the old capitalism is *"It takes money to make money!"* Based upon this theme, America has built awesome industrial machinery capable of producing a seemingly endless array of goods and services. In the process, it has seen its people as extensions of that great machinery—whether on the assembly line or in the executive suite. They have performed *"all that money has asked of them"* and, increasingly, they have come up *"empty"*—devoid of any new ideas, deficit in new sources of growth, dissatisfied with the levels of remuneration on their own terms. In short, they have concluded: *"We can't get there from here anymore — we can't make money by simply investing money!"*

In this context, the central theme of the entrepreneurially driven, free-enterprise global marketplace is this: *"It takes **New Capital Development** or **NCD**, to create wealth."*

What was needed were the technologies to produce these potentially invaluable ingredients. Carkhuff and Berenson have those technologies — the first systematic technologies that constitute the sources of **NCD** and, in turn, **The Freedom Functions.** Indeed, their vision of **The Freedom Doctrine** is based upon these capital resources.

The Freedom Doctrine is really an extension of *The Continuing American Revolution.* Just as the Constitution created the nation and presented us with an instrument of change to share its power with its citizens politically, so will **The Freedom Doctrine** create and extend the concept of wealth and power and their distribution to all contributors. Just as the Bill of Rights and Civil Rights freed American citizens physically and emotionally to make their contributions, so will **The Freedom Doctrine** free **Global Citizens** intellectually and interdependently to actualize their contributions. Viewing the human mind as the rarest of all materials, **The Freedom Doctrine** enables each person to become the source of new and heretofore untold wealth.

To be sure, Carkhuff and Berenson's vision of **The Freedom Doctrine** is accompanied by **The New Bill of Rights:**

- The rights of all citizens to be empowered to contribute their creative ideas to the new culture;

- The rights of all citizens to process information and make decisions for productive economic and cultural purposes;

- The rights of all citizens to think themselves out of their jobs, trusting that their entrepreneurial initiative will generate new roles and challenges.

There is also **The New Bill of Rights** for corporations:

- The right to capitalize upon thinking as the source of economic value;

- The right to benefit from new ideational breakthroughs by employees;

- The right to trust that investments in **NCD** will be dedicated to economic as well as cultural benefits.

Like the American War of Independence, then, *The New Global Revolution* will begin with the inspiration, commitment, and creative thinking of a few leaders who will transform the vision into a mission. Soon the armies of thinkers from the homes and communities, schools and governments, businesses and marketplaces, economies and cultures, will provide the motivation, perspiration, and, above all, possibilities thinking to accomplish the mission.

Make no mistake about it! **The Freedom Doctrine** is *The New Global Revolution!* Ultimately, it requires a **Declaration of Interdependence:** that every person is interdependent with every other person—production and delivery personnel along with managers, executives, and policymakers; that every organization is interdependent with every other organization—home, school, and government as well as business, that every community and culture is interdependent with every other—producers and consumers alike in the commerce of towns, cities, regions, states, and nations.

We are the army of *Freedom-Builders.* We are at war to free ourselves of the restrictive burdens of our old cultures. Our weapons are our thinking skills. Our destiny is in our minds!

Some Amendments

There are those who believe that *Freedom-Building* is merely a reaction to terrorism. This could not be further from the truth.

We were on the *Freedom-Building* course on September 10, 2001. We will continue on this course. *Freedom-Building* is an affirmation of the human spirit. **Global Freedom** is already in the minds and hearts and souls of civilized people everywhere.

Indeed, **Global Freedom** is the mission of **The Freedom Doctrine** that is called *America:* to help build a healthy and prosperous world as we have built our own nation and its people.

To be sure, just as it was in our spiritual legacy, so it is now in our spiritual destiny to be helpers and healers! To help create a global vision of both *The Spirit and Science of Freedom!*

To sum, intentionality is the guiding philosophy of Carkhuff and Berenson and **The New Science of Possibilities** and the sciences and technologies that it generates: to go by intentionality to places we have never been and build by dimensionality our homes and communities and cultures and nations on this spacecraft we lovingly call *Planet Earth.*

With apologies to Robert Browning:

> *Ah, but a nation's grasp must achieve its*
> *reach, or what's our brainpower for?*

APPENDICES

A. Milestones in The Possibilities Science of Carkhuff and Berenson

B. Summary of Contributions to New Capital Market Revolutions

C. Selected References for Freedom-Building Applications

Appendix A

Milestones in The Possibilities Science of Carkhuff and Berenson

Helping and Human Relations

1963 Truax and Carkhuff form *Group Therapy Research* group, universities of Kentucky and Wisconsin, for the study of all counseling and psychotherapeutic relationships. Research validates the potency of the core dimensions of empathy, respect, genuineness, concreteness, and other dimensions.

1964 Truax and Carkhuff's work on *Toward Effective Counseling and Psychotherapy* summarizes "breakthrough" research on the effective ingredients in counseling and psychotherapeutic relationships. Research establishes the power of core dimensions in training and practice of counseling and psychotherapy.

1965 Berenson, Carkhuff and Aspy form *HRD Research Group,* University of Massachusetts, for the study of all **Human Resource Development (HRD).** Research identified the methodologies for the acquisition, application, and transfer of core dimensions of all helping and human relationships.

1966 Berenson and Carkhuff's work on *Sources of Gain in Counseling and Psychotherapy* introduces sources of **HRD.** Research identifies the most powerful sources of learning and growth: didactic, modeling, experiential, and differential reinforcement.

1967 Carkhuff and Berenson's *Beyond Counseling and Therapy* introduces first systematic eclectic approaches to **HRD.** Research establishes the sources of differential treatment complementing the core dimensions: psychoanalytic, behavioristic, trait-and-factor, client-centered, and existential.

1968   Griffin, Berenson, and Carkhuff create the first *Center for HRD* at American International College, Springfield, Massachusetts, for the training, practice, and research of all sources of human and community resource development: parenting, education, higher education, governance, business, and industry.

1969   Carkhuff's *Helping and Human Relations* introduces the first systematic **Interpersonal Communication Skills Technologies.** Research establishes attending, responding, personalizing, and initiating dimensions as the critical ingredients in training and practice in helping and human relations.

Human Resource Development

1970   Creation of *Carkhuff Institute of Human Technology and Applied Sciences*, Amherst, Massachusetts, dedicated to research and development in human, information, and organizational resource development in both the public and private sectors.

1971   Carkhuff's *The Development of Human Resources* is the first book to introduce the sources of individual **HRD:** didactic, experiential, modeling, and reinforcement sources of learning.

1972   Carkhuff's *Art of Helping* introduces a series presenting the first systematic interpersonal helping skills: attending, responding, personalizing, and initiating, along with the complementary skills of goaling, decision making, problem solving, and program development and implementation.

1973   Berenson's work on *Confrontation* introduces comprehensive research validating responsive and initiative interpersonal dimensions. Research concludes that confrontation is never necessary and never sufficient, yet in the presence of a high-level functioning helper, it may be efficient.

1974   Berenson creates the first *Human Technology Curriculum* at American International College, Springfield, Massachusetts. It is based upon emerging **New Capital Development** technologies: human, information, and organization.

1975   Aspy and Roebuck create the *National Consortium for Humanizing Education*, Northeastern Louisiana University and Texas Women's College. Research establishes the primacy of empathic relating as the prepotent source of teaching and learning.

1976   Carkhuff and Berenson's *Teaching as Treatment* introduces psychological education as the preferred mode of all **HRD:** training or empowering helpees of all kinds in the skills they require for functioning productively.

1977   Carkhuff, Berenson, and Berenson create the first systematic *Teaching and Learning Technologies:* interpersonal relating, content development, content organization, teaching delivery, and learning process. These are published in the *Skills of Teaching* series.

1978   Anthony, Cohen, and Cohen create the *Center for Research and Training in Mental Health,* for applications of helpers skills training and "teaching as treatment" at Boston University. Their work is published in *Principles of Psychiatric Rehabilitation.*

1979   Carkhuff, Fisher, and Friel create the *Instructional System Design* and *Training Delivery Systems.* They present instructional intervention design: establishing productivity goals, analyzing contextual tasks, specifying training objectives, developing training content, planning training delivery.

Human and Information Capital Development

1980 Creation of *Human Technology, Inc.*, a private-sector corporation dedicated to human, information, and organizational capital development.

1981 Carkhuff's *Toward Actualizing Human Potential* operationalizes **HRD** technologies for individual development with the formula for **HRD**—physical, emotional, intellectual:

$$\text{HRD} \longleftrightarrow \text{P} \cdot \text{E}^2 \cdot \text{I}^3$$

Physical energizes. Emotional catalyzes. Intellectual actualizes.

1982 Carkhuff's work on *Interpersonal Skills and Human Productivity* summarizes two decades of **HRD** research involving more than 150 studies of more than 160,000 people. Research establishes the effectiveness of relating skills for living, learning, and working functions.

1983 Carkhuff's *Sources of Human Productivity* defines the first systematic technologies for organizational productivity. It presents the first models for organizational productivity systems: human, information, and organizational capital development.

1984 Carkhuff's *The Exemplar* defines the first systematic technologies for individual performance. It presents models for "thinking better" to complement "working smarter" and "working harder" skills programs.

1985   Carkhuff's work on *Human Processing and Human Productivity* introduces the first systematic individual, interpersonal, and organizational processing systems. Highlight is the introduction of the breakthrough **S–P–R** generative thinking skills.

1986   Carkhuff technologies produce the first *Productive Thinking Systems:* exploring by analyzing current operating procedures, understanding by synthesizing productive operating principles, acting by operationalizing productive operating programs.

1987   Carkhuff's technologies produce first *Interdependent Processing Systems:* interdependent processing functions, interpersonal processing components, individual processing systems.

Carkhuff is recognized by **The Institute for Scientific Information** as:

- One of the *Most-Cited Social Scientists in the 20th Century;*
- Author of three of the most-referenced scientific texts, including *Helping and Human Relations (Volumes I and II),* and *Toward Effective Counseling and Psychotherapy.*

New Capital Development

1988   Carkhuff's *The Age of the New Capitalism* introduces the **New Capital Development,** or **NCD,** ingredients in the equation for generating wealth: mechanical, information, human, organizational, and marketplace capital development.

1989   Carkhuff's *Empowering* introduces requirements and technologies for generating **NCD: MCD, OCD, HCD, ICD, mCD.**

1990   *Carkhuff Thinking Systems, Inc.,* or *CTS,* is dedicated to R&D of all processing systems: marketplace, organizational, human, information, mechanical.

1991   R&D yields possibilities processing models for **ICD:** phenomenal, vectorial, dimensional, operational, conceptual.

1992   R&D yields possibilities processing models for **HCD** — physical, emotional, intellectual:

$$\text{HCD} \longleftrightarrow P \cdot E^2 \cdot I^5$$

1993   R&D yields possibilities processing models for **OCD:** goaling, inputting, processing, planning, outputting.

1994   R&D yields possibilities processing models for **MCD:** generating, innovating, commercializing, commoditizing, attenuating.

1995   R&D yields possibilities processing models for **Community Capital Development,** or **CCD:** business, governance, higher education, schools, homes, and neighborhoods.

1996   R&D yields possibilities processing models for **Governance Capital Development,** or **GCD:** free and direct democratic governance.

1997   R&D yields possibilities processing models for **Economic Capital Development,** or **ECD:** entrepreneurially driven, free enterprise economies.

1998   R&D yields possibilities cultural processing models for **Cultural Capital Development,** or **CCD':** interdependent relating cultures.

1999   R&D yields possibilities processing models for **Educational Capital Development,** or **ECD'**— *"The New 3Rs" Curriculum: Relating, Representing, Reasoning.*

Possibilities Science Applications

2000   **CTS** continues R&D in possibilities science and publishes the following:

- *The New Science of Possibilities, Volume I. The Processing Science:* relating, empowering, and freeing functions.

- *The New Science of Possibilities, Volume II. The Processing Technologies:* inductive, deductive, generative, hybrid, paradigmatic, and paradigmetric processing systems.

- *The Possibilities Organization:* leadership, marketing, resource integration, technology, and production.

- *The Possibilities Leader:* information relating and representing; individual, interpersonal, and interdependent processing.

- *Human Possibilities:* physical, emotional, interpersonal, informational, individual, interpersonal, and interdependent processing.

- *The Possibilities Mind:* universality, virtuality, interdependency, asymmetry, operationality, unequality, nesting, encoding, rotation, and changeability.

2001   **CTS** continues R&D in applications of possibilities science:

- R&D yields models, systems, and technologies in *Possibilities Education:*

  - *Possibilities Education Models*
  - *Possibilities Schools Systems*
  - *Possibilities Teacher Technologies*
  - *Possibilities Learner Technologies*
  - *"The New 3Rs" Curriculum*

- Carkhuff develops and presents sources of *Globalization and Leadership*:
  - *Interdependent Cultural Relating*
  - *Free-Enterprise Market Economics*
  - *Direct Democratic Governance*

2002
- Carkhuff, Berenson, and Cannon create *The New Capital Development Group,* dedicated to applications of possibilities science to *Freedom-Building:*
  - *The New Science of Freedom-Building*
  - *The Possibilities Culture*
  - *The Possibilities Economics*
  - *The Possibilities Market*
  - *The Possibilities Business*
  - *The Possibilities Community*

2003
- Carkhuff, Berenson, and Owen create *Freedom Doctrine International.*

APPENDIX B

Summary of Contributions to New Capital Market Revolutions

Contributions to Market Revolutions by Carkhuff and Berenson

1960s • First *Interpersonal Skills (IPS) Systems. IPS* comprises an
estimated one-half of all management training programs.
Sources: *Beyond Counseling and Therapy,* 1967
Helping and Human Relations, 1969

1970s • First *Human Resource Development (HRD) Systems. HRD*
emphasized emotional, motivational, and interpersonal relating
for team-building.
Sources: *Sources of Gain in Counseling and Psychotherapy,* 1967
The Development of Human Resources, 1971

1980s • First *Human Capital Development (HCD) Systems. HCD*
emphasizes intellectual functioning: individual, interpersonal,
interdependent processing.
Sources: *Toward Actualizing Human Potential,* 1981
Human Processing and Human Productivity, 1986

• First *Information Capital Development (ICD) Systems. ICD*
emphasizes information modeling: conceptual, operational,
dimensional, vectorial, phenomenal.
Sources: *Sources of Human Productivity,* 1983
The Exemplar, 1984

1990s • First *Organizational Capital Development (OCD) Systems.
OCD* is generated by organizational alignment with marketplace
positioning.
Sources: *The Possibilities Leader,* 2000
The Possibilities Organization, 2000

• First *Marketplace Capital Development (MCD) Systems. MCD*
is generated by differentiated positioning in the marketplace.
Sources: *Empowering,* 1989
The GICCA Curve — The Possibilities Marketplace, 2002

2000s • First *New Capital Development (NCD) Systems. NCD* is the interdependent processing of all capital development systems: **MCD, OCD, HCD, ICD, mCD.**
Sources: *The Age of the New Capitalism,* 1988
The Possibilities Economics, 2002

• First *Integrated Process Development (IP⁵D) Systems. IP⁵D* is the interdependent processing of all systems: positioning, partnering, people, processing, products.
Sources: *IP⁵D — Integrated Process Development: The Possibilities Business in The Possibilities Economy,* 2002
The Possibilities Culture, 2002

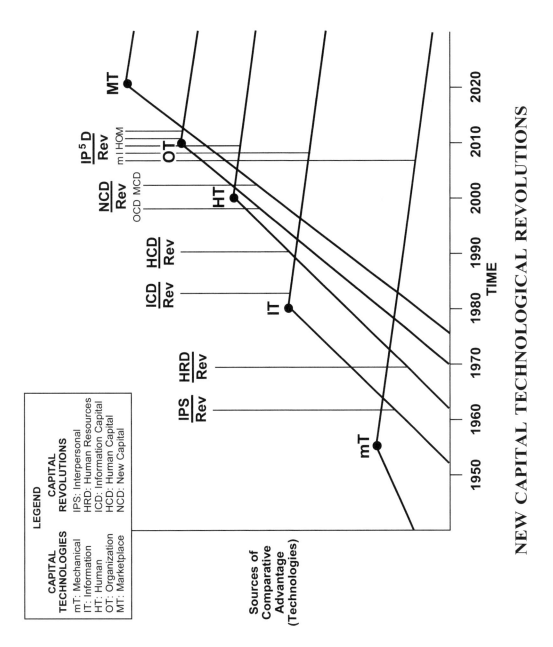

NEW CAPITAL TECHNOLOGICAL REVOLUTIONS

APPENDIX C

Selected References for Freedom-Building Applications

Helping and Human Relations

Anthony, W. A. *The Principles of Psychiatric Rehabilitation.* Baltimore, MD: University Park Press, 1979.

Anthony, W. A., Cohen, M., Farkas, M., and Gagne, C. *Psychiatric Rehabilitation.* Boston, MA: Center for Psychiatric Rehabilitation, 2001.

Berenson, B. G. and Carkhuff, R. R. *Sources of Gain in Counseling and Psychotherapy.* Amherst, MA: HRD Press, 1967.

Berenson, B. G. and Mitchell, K. M. *Confrontation.* Amherst, MA: HRD Press, 1974.

Carkhuff, R. R. *Helping and Human Relations. Volume I. Selection and Training.* New York: Holt, Rinehart & Winston, 1969.

Carkhuff, R. R. *Helping and Human Relations. Volume II. Practice and Research.* New York: Holt, Rinehart & Winston, 1969.

Carkhuff, R. R. *The Art of Helping.* Amherst, MA: HRD Press, 1972.

Carkhuff, R. R. and Berenson, B. G. *Beyond Counseling and Therapy.* New York: Holt, Rinehart & Winston, 1967.

Carkhuff, R. R. and Berenson, B. G. *Teaching as Treatment.* Amherst, MA: HRD Press, 1976.

Truax, C. B. and Carkhuff, R. R. *Toward Effective Counseling and Psychotherapy.* Chicago: Aldine, 1967.

Human and Information Capital Development

Aspy, D. N., Aspy, C. B., and Roebuck, F. N. *The Third Century in American Education.* Amherst, MA: HRD Press, 1984.

Aspy, D. N., and Roebuck, F. N. *Kids Don't Learn From People They Don't Like.* Amherst, MA: HRD Press, 1978.

Carkhuff, R. R. *The Development of Human Resources.* New York: Holt, Rinehart & Winston, 1971.

Carkhuff, R. R. *Toward Actualizing Human Potential.* Amherst, MA: HRD Press, 1981.

Carkhuff, R. R. *IPS — Interpersonal Skills and Human Productivity.* Amherst, MA: HRD Press, 1983.

Carkhuff, R. R. *Sources of Human Productivity.* Amherst, MA: HRD Press, 1983.

Carkhuff, R. R. *The Exemplar.* Amherst, MA: HRD Press, 1984.

Carkhuff, R. R. *Human Processing and Human Productivity.* Amherst, MA: HRD Press, 1986.

Carkhuff, R. R. and Fisher, S. *Instructional System Design. Volumes I and II.* Amherst, MA: HRD Press, 1984.

Carkhuff, R. R. and Pierce, R. M. *Training Delivery Skills. Volumes I and II.* Amherst, MA: HRD Press, 1984.

Possibilities Science and New Capital Development

Berenson, B. G. and Carkhuff, R. R. *Psychology of Possibilities.* Amherst, MA: HRD Press, 2003.

Berenson, B. G. and Carkhuff, R. R. *The Possibilities Mind.* Amherst, MA: HRD Press, 2001.

Berenson, B. G. and Carkhuff, R. R. *The Philosophy of Possibilities Science.* Amherst, MA: HRD Press, in press, 2003.

Carkhuff, R. R. *The Age of The New Capitalism.* Amherst, MA: HRD Press, 1988.

Carkhuff, R. R. *Empowering.* Amherst, MA: HRD Press, 1989.

Carkhuff, R. R. and Berenson, B. G. *The New Science of Possibilities. Volume I. The Processing Science.* Amherst, MA: HRD Press, 2000.

Carkhuff, R. R. and Berenson, B. G. *The New Science of Possibilities. Volume II. The Processing Technologies.* Amherst, MA: HRD Press, 2000.

Carkhuff, R. R. and Berenson, B. G. *Human Capital Development. Volume I. HCD Models.* Amherst, MA: HRD Press, 2003.

Carkhuff, R. R. and Berenson, B. G. *Human Capital Development. Volume II. HCD Technologies.* Amherst, MA: HRD Press, 2003.

Carkhuff, R. R. and Berenson, B. G. *The Principles of Possibilities Science.* Amherst, MA: HRD Press, 2003.

Possibilities Science and Freedom-Building

Carkhuff, R. R. *Human Possibilities.* Amherst, MA: HRD Press, 2000.

Carkhuff, R. R., Aspy, D. N., Benoit, D., and Griffin, A. H. *The Possibilities Schools Series.* Amherst, MA: HRD Press, in press, 2003.

Carkhuff, R. R., and Berenson, B. G. *The Possibilities Leader.* Amherst, MA: HRD Press, 2000.

Carkhuff, R. R., and Berenson, B. G. *The Possibilities Organization.* Amherst, MA: HRD Press, 2000.

Carkhuff, R. R., and Berenson, B. G. *The Possibilities Economics.* Amherst, MA: HRD Press, 2002.

Carkhuff, R. R., Berenson, B. G., and Griffin, A. H. *The Possibilities Culture.* Amherst, MA: HRD Press, 2002.

Carkhuff, R. R., Carkhuff, C. J., and Cohen, B. *IP⁵D—Integrated Process Development: The Possibilities Business in the Possibilities Economy.* Amherst, MA: HRD Press, 2002.

Carkhuff, R. R., Carkhuff, C. J., and Kelly, J. T. *The GICCA Curve: The Possibilities Marketplace.* Amherst, MA: HRD Press, 2002.

Carkhuff, R. R., Griffin, A. H., and Berenson, B. G. *The Possibilities Community.* Amherst, MA: HRD Press, 2002.

Carkhuff, R. R. and Berenson, B. G., and Associates. *The Freedom Doctrine—The Architecture for Global Freedom.* Amherst, MA: HRD Press, 2003.